TWAYNE'S WORLD AUTHORS SERIES

A Survey of the World's Literature

Sylvia E. Bowman, Indiana University

GENERAL EDITOR

GREECE

Mary P. Gianos, Detroit Institute of Technology

Editor

Dionysios Solomos

(TWAS 193)

TWAYNE'S WORLD AUTHORS SERIES (TWAS)

The purpose of TWAS is to survey the major writers—novelists, dramiatists, historians, poets, philosophers, and critics—of the nations of the world. Among the national literatures covered are those of Australia, Canada, China, Eastern Europe, France, Germany, Greece, India, Italy, Japan, Latin America, the Netherlands, New Zealand, Poland, Russia, Scandinavia, Spain, and the African nations, as well as Hebrew, Yiddish, and Latin Classical literatures. This survey is complemented by Twayne's United States Authors Series and English Authors Series.

The intent of each volume in these series is to present a critical-analytical study of the works of the writer; to include biographical and historical material that may be necessary for understanding, appreciation, and critical appraisal of the writer; and to present all material in clear, concise English—but not to vitiate the scholarly content of the work by doing so.

Dionysios Solomos

By M. BYRON RAIZIS

Southern Illinois University

Twayne Publishers, Inc.   : :   New York

PA
5616
.S6
Z85

To the memory of
George S. Raizis

Preface

Dionysios Solomos is more than a National Poet to the Greek people. He is a cultural phenomenon, a symbol of the spiritual rebirth of Modern Greece, and, perhaps above all, the Greek Bard of freedom and humanism.

Not only were writers of subsequent generations inspired or influenced by Solomos's achievement, but a substantial number of artists in other creative fields found inspiration in his verse. The famous Exposition, organized by the French Institute of Athens in 1957, presented dozens of names of great Greek artists (painters, sculptors, engravers, composers, dramatists,) who produced art inspired by the poetry of Solomos; for example, that of Nicholas Ghyzis whose celebrated painting, *Glory,* now kept at the National Gallery in Munich, owes its realization to an epigram of the Zantiot poet.

The beginning of Solomos's "Hymn to Liberty," which has become the National Anthem of Greece, has been sung with patriotic fervor on all sorts of occasions for more than a century. Solomos's works are taught in educational institutions, ranging from elementary school to universities; and most lovers and scholars of Modern Greek culture feel it their duty to write a book or article on the bilingual poet. But the Greek does not usually learn about his national poet in school or from books. Even before learning the alphabet most youngsters know by heart and sing several of his immortal lyrics and even stanzas of the "Hymn."

Solomos's *Complete Works* have been published, and reprinted, over one dozen times since his death; and the number of books, articles, essays, dissertations, and other Solomoniana keeps growing steadily. Scholarly works on Solomos in Greek, Italian, French, English, German, Dutch, Rumanian, and several other languages approach the one-thousand mark.

I read with delight, as well as apprehension, Sir Romilly Jenkins' youthful book on Solomos. The style and many critical insights delighted me. Yet the numerous factual inaccuracies, biases, and unsound conclusions in it inspired me to write about Solomos's work from the viewpoint of a comparatist, and to try to present a comprehensive and up-to-date study of the poet and his work for the benefit of the English-speaking public.

Many works of Solomos have been repeatedly translated into most major languages, sometimes competently, sometimes not. My cherished hope is that this present study may attract attention to Solomos and perhaps inspire artistic translators to make some of his greatest works available in good modern versions. Also, scholars in Romanticism, and comparatists, may find Solomos's contributions to Greek and European culture worthy of examination and comment.

This book is divided into twelve chapters, each with several subdivisions. Chapters 1, 2, 3, and 5 deal with Solomos's life; the dramatic events of the Greek Revolution of 1821; and the social, political, and cultural milieu in the Heptanese and in Greece, in the early nineteenth century. Chapter 4 is devoted to the "education" of the poet and to the formulation of his theory of poetry. Chapters 6, 7, 8, 9, 10, and 11 examine, chronologically, Solomos's development as a poet and prose writer, in both Greek and Italian. The last chapter concentrates on the impact of Solomos on the literature and culture of modern Greece.

I am deeply grateful for the advice and suggestions I received from Solomos scholars, such as Dr. E. Kriaras and Dr. L. Polites, professors emeriti at the University of Thessaloniki (Salonica); and to Professor Mario Vitti of the University of Palermo. My study and research were also helped considerably by the scholarly publications of Professor N. B. Tomadakis, University of Athens; and by Professor George Zoras, formerly of the Universities of Athens and of Rome. To Professor Mary P. Gianos, editor of the Greek section of the Twayne World Authors Series, I owe many thanks for guidance, patience, and editorial assistance and encouragement.

All verse and prose translations into English were made by the author unless otherwise indicated. These translations may not be reproduced in other publications without the author's permission.

M. BYRON RAIZIS

Southern Illinois University
Carbondale

Contents

Chronology

1798 Dionysios Solomos born in April, in Zante, the natural son of Count Nicholas Solomos and his young maid, Angelica Nikli.

1801 Brother Demetrios born in December.

1807 Count Nicholas marries Angelica on his deathbed, in February. Angelica, widowed, marries Emmanuel Leontarakis in August; gives birth to John in September.

1808 Young Dionysios goes to Italy for his education, under the tutelage of Don Santo Rossi, first at Saint Catherine's Lyceum in Venice, then at the Royal Lyceum of Cremona.

1813 Writes his first Italian verse.

1815 Graduates from Cremona: begins to study law and literature at the University of Pavia. Writes "Gerusalemme Liberata."

1818 Leaves Italy without having completed his doctorate, returns to Zante.

1818 Under the guardianship of Count N. Messalas. Makes friends among local young intellectuals; improvises in Greek and, mostly, in Italian.

1821 The Greek Revolution against Turkish rule begins on March 25.

1822 His *Rime Improvvisate* published in Corfu by L. Strani.

1822 Dionysios meets Spyridon Trikoupis; studies modern Greek literature; writes more and more in Greek.

1823 In May, writes the "Hymn to Liberty," probably the "Dialogue," and begins "Lambros."

1824 The first siege of Missolonghi and Lord Byron's death. Solomos writes the "Lyrical Poem on the Death of Lord Byron" and other poems.

1825 *The Hymn to Liberty* published at Missolonghi, Paris, and London. New British policy, under Sir George Canning, favoring the Greeks. Solomos completes the famous epigram "To Psara."

1826 "The Poisoned Girl" written. The fall of Missolonghi. Begins "The Free Besieged."

1827 Writes "The Dream" and other satires. Naval victory at Navarino.

1828 Moves to Corfu for good and settles in solitude.

1829 Completes the prose plan for "The Woman of Zakynthos" and writes lyrics.

1830 Greece becomes independent; Count John Capo d'Istria governor.

1831 Solomos's first visit to Zante.
1833 The infamous lawsuit against his half-brother John begins. Second visit to Zante. Begins "The Cretan."
1834 Part of "Lambros" published in the *Ionian Anthology*.
1836 Last visit to Zante.
1838 Lawsuit finally won by Dionysios and Demetrios Solomos.
1845 Nicholas Mantzaros composes music for the "Hymn" and other poems. Solomos works on new versions of "The Free Besieged."
1847 Temporarily returns to Italian composition. Works on "Porphyras."
1849 King Othon bestows on Solomos the Golden Cross of the Royal Order of the Savior, Epigram "To Frances Fraser" written and published
1850 Demetrios becomes president of the Ionian Senate. Dionysios consoles him on his daughter's suicide.
1851 British blockade of Greece: "La Navicella Greca" composed.
1854 The Crimean (Eastern) War.
1855 Solomos's health deteriorates.
1857 "The Poisoned Girl" published in the Athenian magazine *Pandora*. Solomos dies on February 21. State funeral and public mourning throughout the Ionian Islands and free Greece.
1859 His *Found Remains* published in Corfu by James Polylas and P. Quartano, with Polylas's famous "Prolegomena."
1864 King George I ascends on the throne of Greece. Queen Victoria cedes the Ionian Islands to Greece.
1865 King George I proclaims Solomos's "Hymn to Liberty" as Greece's national anthem. His remains transferred and buried in Zante.

CHAPTER 1

Early Life and Times

I *A Bard Dies, Another Is Born*

THE YEAR 1798 may be considered a landmark in modern Greek cultural history, for it marks the beginning of a new era, very much as the publication of the *Lyrical Ballads,* the same year, marks the official appearance of Romanticism in English literature. In 1798 the Turkish authorities in Belgrade executed the Greek educator Reghas Pheraios, from Velestino, Thessaly, believing that they were thus putting an end to his revolutionary activities and agitation on behalf of Greek Independence.[1]

The same year, however, a boy was born on the Greek Island of Zakynthos (Zante), to the aged and rich Count Nicholas Solomos and his beautiful teen-aged servant, Angelica Nikli. The boy was recognized by the old count and baptized Dionysios when about two months old. This offspring of an old aristocrat, who was also a shrewd businessman, and a young girl of plebeian status, was to become the Bard of Greek Freedom and the father of modern Greek poetry, if not of literature in general.[2]

The independence which the forty-year-old Reghas preached and celebrated in his revolutionary "War Song" (Thourios) and other patriotic poems and pamphlets, became one of the main sources of poetic inspiration to Dionysios Solomos, and it remained so till the end of his life. To understand Solomos's love for freedom, one has to examine his formative years and the influences exercised on his intellectual and emotional development by various teachers and circumstances.

The Solomos family had migrated to Zante from another Greek island, Crete, when the Turks conquered it in 1669.[3] Unlike the Greek mainland, Crete had escaped Turkish conquest following the fall of Constantinople in May, 1453. Instead, the Italian state of Venice had added it to its possessions, for it was of vital importance to the Venetians' mercantile and navigational interests. There is no doubt that

Cretans of the Solomos family had rendered service to the Venetian administration, on the island and even in Venice itself, and as a reward they were elevated to nobility. This nobility did not imply the same political or military power that it did in other European feudal nations. It was a superior social position closer to what the British called "landed gentry," and was certainly awarded many privileges, most of them actually methods of safe and swift enrichment, such as monopolies. Nicholas Solomos had increased his large fortune and estates substantially through the tobacco monopoly which he handled with skill and shrewdness. In fact, he was known to the populace as "Old Tobacco."[4] The Solomos's title of nobility was recognized by the Venetian authorities in Zakynthos a generation after their settling on the island in 1699, and on various other occasions.[5] Much later, in 1840, the Ionian state, upon the poet's request, ratified the title again.[6] Dionysios was aware of his Cretan Greek origin, and although he used the Italian language most of the time—as did practically all members of the upper classes in the Ionian islands—not even once did he claim to be Italian or refute his Greekness. As a matter of fact, he established the Greek spelling of his name as Solomos, because up to his time it had been variously spelled as Salamon, Salomon, Salamos, and Salomos.[7] Dionysios and all the members of his family were Greek Orthodox Christians and they were baptized, married, and buried according to the Greek Orthodox rites. None of the numerous Italian Neo-Hellenists ever claimed that Solomos was Italian.[8] Yet this ridiculous claim was implied in an uninformed chapter by a popular British historian, Arnold Toynbee.[9]

The Italian language and culture in general remained strong on the Seven Greek Islands of the Ionian Sea—the Heptanese—long after the extinction of the Venetian Republic, in Napoleon's time, and began gradually to fade only after the union of the Heptanese with Greece, in 1864. One century later, traces of this cultural influence can still be found among the descendants of the now completely Hellenized *nobili.*

But Italy was not the only Western European nation which had exerted a cultural influence on the Ionian islands. The end of the eighteenth century found the Heptanese in French hands. In 1798, the year of Dionysios's birth, the French, under General Chabot, were expelled from the islands by a combined Russian and Turkish force. The dual domination that ensued did not last long. In 1807 the Tilsit treaty awarded the islands to Napoleon, who finally lost them to the British in 1815.[10] The British, with the exception of the first high commissioner, administered the Ionian state as a protectorate, allowing it to have its Senate and elected officials and representatives; and, generally speaking, they ruled with a considerable degree of firmness tempered by understanding, especially when London policies were not in conflict with the interests of the Heptanesians or all Greeks in general. Finally, Queen Victoria, in a generous gesture, ceded the islands to Greece when one of her nephews—a young Danish prince— became King George I of the Hellenes, in 1864.

One can immediately appreciate the importance of all this foreign traffic on Kerkyra, Zakynthos, Kephalonia, and the other Ionian islands. Whereas the Greek mainland and the islands of the Aegean sea had solidly remained under the oppressive and almost stultifying control of Turkey, which had reduced most cultural and artistic activities to a minimum, the Ionian Greeks had the benefit of a European presence in their midst, and a relatively free exchange of ideas, which, of course, influenced their outlook. The Greeks under the Turks had become a largely illiterate, superstitious, and leaderless people, for their oppressors had closed most schools and did not encourage initiative or social innovation. For almost four centuries after the conquest of Byzantium (1453), most of the Greek provinces and territories had remained cut off from the rest of Europe, as if separated from it by an iron curtain. The Heptanese was one of the very few Greek territories where the social, political, cultural, and scientific developments in the West could be followed by Greeks—at least by the aristocracy, the privileged classes, the intellectual elite, and the ambitious. Many male offspring of Heptanesian families would go to Italy to study in its universities and then return to their islands to become lawyers, judges, physicians, educators, administrators, editors, and to disseminate the new ideas and manners that they had picked up while in Italy and even France, Germany, and England. In addition to this cultural input, the Heptanesians enjoyed the benefit of many European visitors, especially Italian liberals, who were in trouble in their country because of Napoleonic and other political pressures. Most of these refugees were sincere patriots and, usually, well educated and idealistic humanists. Their influence on the local intelligentsia was profound and was matched only by their love and gratitude for the hospitable Greeks. Dionysios Solomos was fortunate to have one such man as a tutor and companion when a student: the Catholic priest Don Santo Rossi. He also had several other of these emigres as close friends during his adult life.

It is not, then, difficult for one to understand the considerable cultural differences that existed at the time between Greeks belonging to different social strata, as well as those between the inhabitants of Greece proper and those of the Ionian Islands. All groups were well aware of these differences and were contemptuous of their fellow Greeks living under what each group considered an un-Greek and inferior regime. The educated Heptanesians often considered the Greeks from the mainland to be Oriental and uncouth. The latter group returned the compliment by calling the Heptanesians Franks, a derogatory epithet usually bestowed on non-Greeks, Catholics, and foreigners in general—a rough equivalent to the classic term, "barbarian."

These differences in life style and social customs were dramatically manifested in the Greek dialects spoken at the time. Foreign words, and especially Italian and romance ones, had become a legitimate part of the Heptanesian Greek vocabulary. Some Turkish words had similarly seeped into the dialects of the mainland. Adding to this confusion was the conservative, tradition-bound Greek Orthodox Church, which not only had kept alive the almost classical Greek *(koine)* it had been using since its inception, but had been trying, with some success, to propagate as the only written, for the educated and for those who wanted to study, a modern language which was based on the intricate grammar, syntax, and obsolete vocabulary of classical Greek. This artificial language, *katharevousa* (pure), was never normally spoken, and the majority of the populace did not understand it.[11] In other words, when Solomos was born, two languages and several dialects were used in Greece; and Italian and a vernacular local-Greek dialect were used in Zante.

The importance of the language question in Greece of that time cannot be overemphasized, for the existing confusion was one of the main causes of the curtailment of learning and of paucity of literary production. Ironically, Solomos himself—for many, one of the greatest poets of modern Greece—was one of the victims of this phenomenon of polyglossy, as will be seen later.

Among the many and most significant imports from Western Europe were the ideas of the Enlightenment and of the French Revolution in particular. For a brief spell, during the French "protection" of the islands by General Napoleon's Republican Army, the populace *(popolari)* in Zante revolted against the nobles *(nobili)* and burned their official genealogical record, the *Golden Book* (Libro d'Oro), which to them was a hated symbol of a feudal and oppressive establishment. Nor had the Cephalonians and the Corfiots failed to cause trouble for the ruling class, the church, and later, the first lord high commissioner, Thomas Maitland (1816–24), and his subordinates.[12]

A few months after the outbreak of the Greek Revolution on March 25, 1821, there were bloody riots—nearly a full-scale revolt, in Zante—staged by a group of Greek peasants who attempted to kill the crew of an Algerian warship of the Turkish navy that had run aground, and a British detachment which had been ordered to rescue the sailors and preserve British neutrality in the Greco-Turkish conflict. Both sides then committed senseless atrocities, but the repressive measures of the British following this episode at Ipsolitho succeeded in producing deep resentment and even hatred among the Greeks, including the young Dionysios Solomos.[13]

The British had acted in accordance with the principles of the Holy Alliance to which they were committed. The Greeks, however, and perhaps rightly so, considered the overreaction of their "protectors" as provocative and actually pro-Turkish. It took a long time for the calming of emotions, even on the part of Solomos, and only a complete change in British policies under Sir George Canning, in 1825, succeeded in healing the rift and reestablishing a traditional and mutual understanding and respect between the two Christian nations—Greek and English.

The news, however, that the Greeks had at last revolted against the age-long Ottoman Turkish occupation of Greece, the cradle of Western civilization, had filled with genuine enthusiasm many non-Greeks as well. The Catholic bishop of Zante, Lodovico Scacosz, held a special Thanksgiving service in Saint Mark's cathedral, amid general enthusiasm, which, as was expected, infuriated the British, who demanded his removal. The diplomatic Pope Pius VII transferred the philhellenic clergyman but elevated him by appointing him archbishop of Malta. This moral triumph of the Christian spirit over petty political expediency was long remembered by the Heptanesians (by Solomos in particular) and became a source of inspiration and courage to the rebellious Christians who had to face the might of the Ottoman Turkish Empire and to most of the Heptanesian aristocrats. For it now began to dawn on them that they were Greeks after all.[14]

II *Dionysios's Boyhood in Zante, 1798–1808*

Few details are known about Dionysios's early years, but one can assume that he lived like most children of his social class and age-level in Zante. His father had married Marnetta Kakni, and had begotten six children by her. Only two of the six, Robert (born 1767) and Helen (born 1770), survived infancy, and lived to marry and beget children themselves.[15]

Marnetta's health deteriorated rapidly, and she became an invalid. The still-vigorous "Old Tobacco" then turned his amorous attentions to the young and beautiful Angelica Nikli, his servant. This was not unnatural, nor was it considered especially indecent or improper. One of the prerogatives of aristocrats, everywhere in the world, was the shunning of social custom, or even the law, when it suited them. It must also be said that Angelica was not losing much from such a liaison. On the contrary, her giving birth to young Solomoi—(plural of Solomos)—and to boys especially, could only enhance her social position and her chances for a secure old age. As for the purely moral side of the issue, one need merely recall what was revealed by Lord Byron about Italian morality in *Beppo,* and the ethics of European aristocrats, in general, in *Don Juan* and other works. The Zantiot nobility tolerated such sexual escapades among its ranks, the way its model, the Italian nobility, allowed a husband to suffer the *"cavalier servente"* of his wife. The famous triangle of Lord Byron, Teresa Guiccioli, and Count Alessandro Guiccioli, is a telling example of such arrangements at the time.[16]

Countess Marnetta passed away in 1802; by then Angelica had offered Count Nicholas two sons: Dionysios, in March or April, 1798, and Demetrios in December, 1801. Nicholas lived with her for eleven years, and it is not difficult to imagine that after the countess's death Angelica was, for all practical purposes, her obvious successor. But the old count refrained from marrying her, probably because he feared that if Angelica became Countess Solomos she would become too difficult to handle. Nicholas, however, was fond of his two little sons by her, and not only did he recognize them officially as his own when they were baptized, but he left most of his large fortune to them—at the expense of Robert Solomos. Angelica, on her part, succeeded, virtually at the eleventh hour, to convince old Nicholas to marry her on his deathbed. February 27, 1807, found the former maid a countess with two legitimate male heirs. "Old Tobacco" died the next day.[17]

From his mother, relatives, and neighbors, Dionysios must have learned his first Greek. And this was undoubtedly the language he used with other children and his younger brother. Some old sources have it that one of his Greek tutors was the philologist Anastasios Karavias, a pedantic bachelor as qualified to cultivate young boys' spirits as Henry Fielding's Mr. Thwackum. Also the name of Anthony Martelaos (1754—1819)—a radical intellectual, poet, rebel, and ironically, the son of an Orthodox priest, who had tutored Ugo Foscolo—was linked to Dionysios's Greek education. It is unlikely, however, that the old count, or his hand-picked guardians of the boys, would allow a well-known antinobility radical to tutor Solomos's offspring. Later research has also proved that Karavias had not been to Zante before 1808, when Dionysios left the island. Nicholas B. Tomadakis names an Orthodox priest, Nicholas Kasimatis, as another possible Greek tutor for the boy. One can assume, then, that the boy's Greek schooling was limited, informal, indirect, and of a practical nature.[18] It is known, for instance, that Solomos attended the Greek church regularly and that he enjoyed intoning the "kyrie eleison," and reading the Epistle out loud as part of the service, at the churches of Saint George and Saint Paraskeve.[19]

His Italian tutor, Don Santo Rossi, is the man who influenced young Solomos greatly, not only with his knowledge of Italian and of Latin, but also with his love for freedom and country. Rossi enjoyed the confidence of Solomos's guardian, Count Nicholas Messalas, who apparently was eager to limit the influence of Angelica and her kin on his young wards. When Dionysios was ten, Rossi was asked to accompany the boy to Italy, where he would pursue his formal studies. Demetrios, the younger brother, remained in Zante, but there is no doubt that his guardians saw to it that, as he grew older, he would see less and less of his mother and the rest of her family.[20]

III *The Leontarakis Family*

Old Count Nicholas Solomos had become incapacitated and bed-ridden some time before his death. It so happened then that a young and attractive goldsmith, Emmanuel Leontarakis, was renting a shop located in front of the Solomos townhouse. Beautiful Angelica did not fail to become acquainted with the young tenant, who as a free artisan was socially more than a match for a maid, and eventually became his lover. When her husband of one day died, Angelica was already pregnant with Leontarakis's child. Sensing his good fortune, Emmanuel married Angelica hurriedly, in August, 1807, as soon as circumstances allowed it. In September she gave birth to their son John, but his birth was registered in December.[21] This first child of hers with Leontarakis, a quarter of a century later was to cause great trouble to his half-brothers, his own family, and was to force Dionysios to face a psychic experience from which it is remarkable that he emerged virtually unscathed.

Meanwhile, the count's eldest and legitimate son, Robert Solomos, furious because his father left practically everything to little Dionysios and Demetrios, sued for his part of the estate. The case almost turned to scandal because Robert demanded that Angelica be confined to a convent so that the date of her child's birth could be ascertained. Robert, knowing his father's condition the last months before his death, believed that he could convince the court that Angelica was a girl of loose morals and that all her sons, not only John, had been conceived in adultery; he hoped, then, to recover all of the fortune as the only legitimate Count Solomos.[22]

This was not an easy affair, however, because the boys' two guardians did not wish to stain the memory of the deceased count, nor was the Leontarakis couple willing to take the convent test. A compromise was then reached, leaving all parties satisfied, as Robert received a good chunk of the estate. Thus, the ten-year-old Dionysios and his younger brother were spared a humiliation and a life of destitution. But the ghost of their parents' anomalous marital status and love life was destined to reappear and haunt them in the future.

IV *Studies in Italy, 1808–1818*

In 1808 Don Santo Rossi took Dionysios to Venice and enrolled him at Saint Catherine's Lyceum. The discipline and general atmosphere in this boarding school were too much for the young Greek. Used to a considerable amount of freedom and the carefree life of most juveniles on a Greek island, Dionysios revolted. Rossi then took him to his own town, Cremona, where, under his benevolent supervision, Dionysios pursued his secondary education in the local lyceum and was graduated with distinction, in 1815, winning a prize in rhetoric and just missing one in another subject.[23]

Among his teachers in Cremona, Giovanni Pini, a classicist and a liberal, seems to have taught the young Greek much about Latin poetry and freedom as well. Impressed by the first Latin and Italian verse, usually translations, that Solomos wrote as school exercises—as did Byron and Shelley when pupils—the Italian told the boy: "Greek, you will cause our Monti to be forgotten" *(Greco, tu farai dimenticare il nuostro Monti).*[24] Another great teacher was Hellenist Bernardo Bellini, who later published his recollections of Solomos in a note to a long poem (1841). The boy must have learned at least the rudiments of Greek from Bellini to whom, as a fair exchange, he taught the contemporary pronunciation of the language. Bellini was proud of his young tutor and pupil and remembered him with pleasure when, years later, Count John Capo d'Istria—who became the first governor of free Greece—complimented his pronunciation and fluency in Greek.[25] These two educators apparently aroused Solomos's interest in Homer, Virgil, Dante, Petrarch, and other great poets and helped him appreciate the magic of great verse.

The fall of 1815 found the seventeen-year-old Dionysios a freshman at the University of Pavia studying law. Two years later Solomos passed his preliminary examinations, then attended for a third year and received his certificate. He did not, however, register for the traditional fourth, and final, year to earn his degree and the title of "doctor of jurisprudence."[26]

From his letters to his mother and brother in this period we learn that he felt nostalgic about his native country and that he had missed his mother and relatives greatly. In one of these brief communications he counsels Demetrios to be a nice and obedient boy. In others he inquires after the health of Angelica's father, "that bright old man"; his stepfather, Emmanuel, and the other children. In still another he triumphantly announces his decision to return home in a year's time. All these letters show a genuine and deep affection for his mother and relatives. Solomos's love for his mother, undoubtedly increased in their long separation, tended to idealize her in his innocent and impressionable imagination.[27] There is no doubt that Dionysios was tormented at the thought that Count Messalas was not encouraging much contact between Demetrios and Angelica, for on many occasions he urged the boy to visit their mother.

Dionysios used to joke about his training in law, saying that it was only because of his professors' kindness that he was allowed to graduate. In reality, however, we know that he was far more interested in the humanities, literature, and philosophy and that he attended the lectures of several distinguished professors in these disciplines. Giovanni Canna reported that Solomos had heard the lectures of Elia Giardini, of Ignazio Beretta, the Hellenist Matteo Butturini, as well as those of professors Tamburini, Giordani, Resi, and others.[28]

During his stay in the north of Italy, Venice, and the country near

Milan, Solomos met, and was on familiar terms with the famous Classicist poet and translator of Homer, Vincenzo Monti (1754–1828). All biographers of Solomos recount the time that the two of them were discussing Perticari's interpretation of a passage in Dante's *Inferno*. The young Greek could not accept the meaning as explained by the critic. Monti, on the contrary, accepted it without hesitation. "Nobody should rationalize so much," Monti rebuked the youth, "one should feel, feel." Solomos then retorted that the mind must first conceive with strength, what the heart will then fervently feel.[29] Monti was right in that particular instance, but Solomos's answer is indicative of his own understanding of the fundamental nature of poetic inspiration. Feeling was important, but it could not suffice without the intervention of reason, which would limit its possibly excessive manifestations and would add the appropriate intellectual dimensions to the poem.

Solomos became vividly interested in the theory and works of the Italian Romantic authors Giovanni Torti (1774–1852) and Alessandro Manzoni (1785–1873). Torti was a good friend of Solomos, and through him and the Greek historian Andreas Mustoxydis, the young Greek may have been introduced to Manzoni in Milan. Torti was the author of what was considered the Second Romantic Manifesto. In his four verse essays (1818), Torti popularized ideas about literature, shared by Manzoni, which laid emphasis on nature, sentiment, faith, morality, imagination, wisdom—all of them presented in idealized forms.[30] This special brand of Italian Romanticism apparently appealed to Solomos and inspired him, for he had a low opinion of the artificial ornamentation and rhetoric of Neoclassic, pseudo-romantic, artful expression like Monti's.

Manzoni, who was to make a great reputation in 1827 with his folkloric novel *The Betrothed* (I Promessi Sposi), began publishing his *Sacred Hymns* (Inni Sacri) in 1815. This collection of idealistic poetic effusions on Christianity not only became a source of inspiration to the young Greek but also served as a direct model for imitation. Manzoni's *Ode to Napoleon,* his other *Hymns,* the drama *Adelchi,* and other works were also read and appreciated by Solomos. Manzoni, moreover, was a friend of the famous French folklorist and philhellene Charles Claude Fauriel, who introduced him to the wealth and greatness of popular culture.[31] Folk songs and other such "unsophisticated" literary forms were *de rigueur* on the Continent among Romantic intellectuals, and the success of Robert Burns's poems and songs—and earlier the "Ossianic" creations—in England proved the indisputable artistic value of traditional, ethnic, and folkloric literature.

Later in his life Solomos was to collaborate with Fauriel. But perhaps the ideas of this Frenchman, and the example of Manzoni, were the first stimuli which soon made Dionysios discover the possibilities of the Greek popular (demotic) culture as a vehicle and a source for literary creation.

Most of the Italian poems composed by Solomos were sonnets modeled on those of the Italian sonneteers known as the "Arcadians,"[32] and other practitioners of the genre in Italian, including Monti. Solomos never wrote a sonnet in Greek. His imitators and disciples, however, wrote some of the best Greek sonnets, and in general they popularized this genre in Greek.

What can be inferred about the intellectual awakening of Solomos in Italy is that he absorbed the contemporary Italian culture, and the European spirit in general, mastered them, and became their exponent in the Greek world, not simply in the shape or form that he found them, but in the form that could become genuinely Greek.

Whatever in European or Italian Romanticism was decadent or alien to the aspirations of a newly emerging nation, with a renewed culture, Solomos refrained from introducing into Greek lore. Although he was familiar with the "Graveyard school" of poetry in its Continental as well as in its English manifestations—Solomos had great respect for the poet of *The Tombs* (I Sepolchri, 1806), his fellow Zantiot Ugo Foscolo[33]—he did not see fit to transplant this kind of art in the emerging cultural climate in Greece. And one can say that with so many deaths of close relatives and friends Solomos would have been completely justified had he done so. But this was not what Greece needed then. The imitative contemporary and later Romantic poets in Greece proper, though, were in no position to make such subtle artistic distinctions, and became sheepish imitators of the European sobbing and lamenting versifiers of melancholy.

Solomos was instinctively aware of the cultural needs of his nation and began to visualize clearly his position as a potential national bard. To fulfill this role he needed the idealism of Italian Romanticism, love of country, faith in God, and respect for the morally beautiful and noble in mankind. "Faith and Motherland" (Pistis kai Patris) became the silent motto of Solomos. The problem that now lay ahead was that of the choice of the right poetic vehicle.

Giuseppe Montani was another close friend and fellow student of Solomos, and, according to James Polylas, he was an influential one. Montani was a "sincere and fervent lover of Truth and Righteousness," and his idealism might have affected Solomos's inner world.[34] As

Solomos was returning to Zante, via Venice, Montani sent him a long, affectionate letter therein expressing his sorrow at the Greek's departure. Among other things, the future literary critic mentioned that patriotism would become a source of inspiration to Solomos, who would express "true and brave sentiments" and would arouse strong emotions with his verse. Nor did Montani fail to compare the political situation and the lack of true freedom in Italy and the Heptanese. He considered the British protection of the latter as a more benevolent form of slavery, with some degree of autonomy, than the foreign and oppressive rule in Italy.[35]

Solomos left Italy with his heart and mind filled with feelings of gratitude and admiration. More than three decades later he wrote in one of his last works, the Italian poem "The Small Greek Ship" (La Navicella Greca), that he went to Italy a "barbarian" but he had not come back one.[36] This paraphrased echo from one of Horace's Odes about the effects of a Greek journey on him, is quite indicative of the role that the Greek intellectual had been called to play by destiny. Reversing the traffic of cultural influences, Solomos would now introduce to Greece the lights of the West, the French Enlightenment, the Italian idealism, and the lore of Europe in general.

CHAPTER 2

The Making of a Poet

I *The Decade in Zante, 1818–1828*

ZAKYNTHOS, despite its limited size and population, had always succeeded in maintaining the semblance of a cultured atmosphere![1] In addition to Solomos and Andreas Kalvos, another contemporary Greek poet of patriotism and freedom, the island was the birthplace of Ugo Foscolo (1778–1827), a half-Greek poet who distinguished himself in the pantheon of Italian Romanticism and, among other things, had lived some time in England and translated into Italian Laurence Sterne's *Sentimental Journey* (1813). Zante had produced a considerable number of Zantiot intellectuals who used to get together often and hold long and heated discussions on topical issues, or simply entertain themselves at parties with impromptu recitations, songs, and humorous stories. The natural charm, education, and talent of Dionysios soon impressed this elite group, and before long he was its dominant personality.

Some of Solomos's friends and companions at those convivial gatherings and typically Greek symposia were Anthony Matesis (1794–1875), a poet, and later author of *The Basil Plant* (1830); George Tertsetis (1800–74), who later became a prominent judge in Athens and a writer of verse and memoirs; Count Paul Merkatis (1771–1854); Nicholas Luntzis (1798–1885); Diamantopoulos; Kokkinis; Emmanuel Leontarakis—the second husband of Solomos's mother—the two physicians Dionysios Roidis and Dionysios Tayiapieras; Andreas Komiotis, a member of the secret "Society of Friends" (Philike Hetairia); and the Italian scholar Gaetano Grassetti, who later translated and edited Solomos's "Hymn to Liberty" and taught at the Ionian Academy (university) in Corfu.[2]

Though most of these men received much more, in the long run, than what they offered Solomos at that stage, their contributions to the making of the young poet should not be neglected. The German-educated Luntzis and his brother, the historian Hermann, later on

25

became the main exponents of contemporary German philosophy and literature to Solomos, for they translated into Italian many German texts at his request. Dr. Tayiapieras, a friend of the multi-talented John Vilaras, was an exponent of democratic principles and, like Vilaras, a dedicated supporter of the demotic (vernacular) language. He also knew Adamantios Koraes and his works and ideas on language. From Tayiapieras Solomos might have heard, for the first time, sound arguments about the Greek language and contemporary literature, in addition to politics. On the other hand, the other practitioner of Hippocrates's science, Roidis, a much older man and the clown of the circle, often became the target of the group's satirical improvisations in verse, as he himself wrote atrocious poems which he considered to be masterpieces.

Fun-loving, light, often frivolous, the Zantiots had a reputation for comic and satiric verse which had recently been enhanced by successful practitioners, such as Nicholas Koutouzis (1741–1813), who was also a painter of icons, and Demetrios Gouzelis (1774–1848), author of the comedy *The Loser* (1790). Following this local tradition, Solomos composed three satires on Roidis, around 1824, which are unique philological specimens of the bilinguality of the poet and his company, and of the ease with which he handled the Greek idiom of Zante, which was studded with Italian words and expressions. At that time, Solomos wrote not less than six Italian poems in a similarly light vein, imitating and ridiculing this unsuccessful doctor and poetaster.[3]

Komiotis might have been the man who first spoke to Solomos about the sacred aspirations of the "Society of Friends": to inspire and organize a general Greek uprising against their Turkish oppressors. Though the names of Dionysios and his brother figure on the list of members of this patriotic society in contemporary Heptanese, no further evidence, let alone proof, of Dionysios's involvement in this idealistic conspiracy has been found.[4] And it is not difficult to explain why.

The society was founded in Odessa, Russia, by Greek intellectuals and businessmen, such as Emmanuel Xanthos and Theodore Tsakaloff, in 1814. After the defeat of Napoleon, these patriots believed that a widespread uprising of the Greeks would be supported by the Russians, who were traditional enemies of Turkey, and who had always tried to pose as protectors of the Christian populations of the Ottoman Empire. The Russians were held in high esteem by many Greeks, since they were the only major power professing the Orthodox Christian faith. In the recent past, under Empress Catherine the Great, a Russian expeditionary fleet had inflicted a series of defeats on the Ottoman navy in the Aegean Sea and had aroused high hopes of freedom among the Greeks, some of whom revolted against the Turks. But the czarina soon lost interest in these operations, and, despite Voltaire's persistent exhortations to become the liberator of Hellas, she abandoned her coreligionists to the avenging fury of the Turks.[5]

Time, however, had healed this wound, and the Greek patriotic Society—now led by a former member of the Czar's cabinet, Count Capo d'Istria, and a brave officer, Prince Alexander Ypsilanti, who had distinguished himself in Russia's wars against Napoleon—was ready to stage the rebellion on two fronts, today's Rumania and the Greek mainland.

Solomos, however, and all Heptanesians were technically British subjects, since the Ionian state was a British protectorate. England had no reason, at the time, to support any liberation movements that were contrary to the principles of the Holy Alliance. Nor was England interested in strengthening Russia's influence in southeastern Europe by weakening Turkey. For the English believed that once Greece became a free state she would become a natural ally of the Orthodox and neighborly Russians. Finally, Czar Alexander I himself did not dare breach his commitment to the Holy Alliance and, at the last moment, refrained from aiding the Greeks.

When Ypsilanti and his small Greek army of volunteers crossed the Turco—Russian border, near the Pruth, in February, 1821, a Russian army was standing by, anxiously waiting for the signal to cross the river and assist the Greeks and other fellow Christians. But they waited in vain, for such a signal never came.

Now, if Solomos, who was not a conspiratorial type, were to have become involved in this affair, directly or indirectly, the immediate result would have been his arrest by the British authorities, confiscation of the family property, loss of nobility title, and harassment of his relatives. As a trained lawyer and a man of contemplative disposition, Solomos knew better than to become involved right away. Also, he had never liked manly sports such as fencing, boxing, and hunting, nor was he trained in active warfare. Moreover, his brother Demetrios was always of a conservative and loyal attitude toward the authorities. Last, but not least, Count Messalas and the other guardians and executors of the Solomos's estate were law-abiding and conservative citizens, so there is no doubt that young Dionysios could not make a decision on his own. According to his father's will, Dionysios was not to become master of his estate until 1822.[6] The violent British reaction during the episode at Ipsolitho, when some Zantiots mistreated some Ottoman sailors—after the outbreak of the revolution—proved that the authorities meant to maintain the English neutrality at any cost.

After this long parenthesis, one may again turn his attention to Dionysios's life at that period. The carefree and happy hours with his interesting and gay friends made up only one side of Solomos's activities—and a small part at that. Solomos, who was extremely fond of nature, would spend hours on solitary walks on the beautiful island, around Akrotiri. We know that he used to visit various picturesque chapels situated around the town. He was a frequent visitor to his uncle Lodovico Strani's villa in the country a few miles from Zante.[7] There he spent endless hours reading, contemplating the exquisite landscape, composing verse or, rather seldom, enjoying the company of friends and relatives.

Like Wordsworth reliving his recollections from earlier visits to a particularly impressive spot, Solomos must have revisited the streets, hills, woods, and beaches that had once been his boyhood playgrounds. A medallion from the pre-Italy period portrays Dionysios as a beautiful boy with large, expressive eyes, radiating with life. One can imagine him, as is often reported, reading the Epistle and chanting in Greek during Sunday and holiday services, or reciting nursery rhymes, or still later winning the first prize in rhetoric while in Cremona. For all his strong sense of personal freedom, Dionysios was never a wild child, nor one given to excessive physical activity. His contemplative and sensitive nature was manifested early. Kairophylas reports that little Dionysios and another boy were once walking in the attractive countryside when the notes from a distant shepherd's pipe interrupted the silence. Dionysios, charmed by the sweetness of the simple melody which merged with the beauty of the landscape, felt a strong sensation in him. He stopped his friend and eagerly asked him: "What do you feel?" "Nothing" was the answer of the surprised companion.[8]

In another characteristic situation the boy Dionysios, with tears in his eyes, is said to have kissed the hand of a young playmate who had done some good act.[9] In still another story Dionysios is reported as having freed a little bird from its cage with the words, "Fly little bird, fly to freedom".[10] Though most of these anecdotes cannot be verified with certainty, the early letters of the young Greek to his mother, to his friends, and many instances in his early verse, show that Solomos was capable of such noble sentiments and actions.

There are early proofs of Solomos's enlightened and liberal ideas, for in February, 1821, Dionysios helped draft, and signed, an official document protesting the reactionary constitution of 1817, and Maitland's highhanded policies.[11] This protest to King George III could have provoked a violent response. But the British crown was more diplomatic now. Maitland's successors tried to win over the Heptanesian aristocracy, and thus isolate the often restless peasantry and bourgeoisie of the islands. This measure had more success than Maitland's brutality. Enlightened and benevolent high commissioners, later on, won over even the hardened heart of Dionysios. Also Sir Frederick North, Lord Guilford (1766–1827), with his genuine philhellenism did much to restore a sense of understanding between the English and the Greeks at that time. Not only did he become a convert to the Greek Orthodox faith, but he would often stroll in the streets of Corfu dressed in the Classical Greek fashion and talking to the inhabitants in their own language.[12] On the serious side, Guilford reorganized and inaugurated officially the Ionian Academy, in 1824, which was founded in 1807. Its more than thirty professors—quite a large number considering the size of the population and the number of students—were to be partly paid from the substantial endowment Lord Guilford left to this first Neo-Hellenic university.[13]

Solomos composed verse honoring this great philhellene. At that time he did not use his title of nobility, and the company he kept with untitled bourgeois and almost radical republicans is an indication of his liberal disposition and humanism in general.

Robert, his half-brother, and Demetrios, his brother, were now both married, and had established themselves in the conservative circle of Zantiot aristocracy. They had no use for Dionysios's liberalism and "inferior" acquaintances, nor would they do anything to displease the British Resident on the island. It was rumored that their haughty and greedy wives were responsible for the creation of petty episodes between Dionysios and the other Solomoi.[14] Though this cannot be ascertained, there is no doubt that some friction began to develop among the Solomos brothers.

II *The First Greek Poems*

While in Italy Dionysios had continued composing Italian poems, often in emulation of the great masters he was studying. "The Destruction of Jerusalem" was the first juvenile but ambitious undertaking around 1815. At the same time he wrote the "Ode for the

First Mass," a favorite poem of his, as well as some other pieces. Back in Zante, Solomos, following the popular tradition, often improvised in Italian, during the convival parties with his friends at the homes of Merkatis, Luntzis, or Leontarakis. The majority of these pieces were sonnets. Thirty of them were collected and published by the poet's uncle, Lodovico Strani, without Dionysios's knowledge, in Corfu, in 1822. The title of the thin volume was *Poetic Improvisations* (Rime Improvvisate), and Strani prefaced them by a kind of epistle dedicatory to Ugo Foscolo, the Zantiot who was then garnering glory as an Italian poet. What is of greater importance in that preface is Strani's statement that Solomos had been trying hard to compose in Greek as well, and create a Greek literary language, and that his recitation of "The Mad Mother," a "very moving and original Greek poem," never failed to fill his audience's eyes with tears.[15]

There is no doubt, then, that during this period Solomos had started to write in Greek, using as linguistic models the popular ballads and demotic songs which he had been hearing in Zante since his return in 1818, and which he must have heard as a boy as well.

In addition to "The Mad Mother," a number of other charming Greek lyrics were written then or a little later: "Eurykome," "To a Maiden," "Anthoula," "Desire," "The Dream," "To Mr. Lodovico Strani," "Anger," "Ode to the Moon," "Granddad's Shadow," "Homer's Shadow," "The Unknown Girl," "The Little Blonde Girl," "The Death of the Shepherd," "To Mr. George de Rossi in England," "To a Dying Friend," "Recollection," and others. Soon many of these lyrics became very popular, for the population understood them and held them as their own, and the Italian-speaking *nobili* were satisfied that they had come from the pen of an aristocrat. Several were set to catchy tunes and were on the lips of all. Solomos's reputation as a Greek poet began to be made. And what is important, these poems became a possession of the people through the oral tradition, for they were never printed immediately, or officially published during Solomos's life. When Spyridon Trikoupis came to Zante to meet him, "Solomos's name was in the mouths of all the people."[16]

III   *Solomos and Trikoupis*

Spyridon Trikoupis (1788–1873) was a young scholar with an English and Continental education, who later became an historian and the father of one of Greece's progressive prime ministers. Lord Guilford had invited him to Zante, late in 1822, and Trikoupis obliged. Solomos was then in one of his periods of self-imposed solitude, far from the city, seeing nobody. But Trikoupis succeeded in visiting Dionysios in his country villa, and the two "Europeanized" Greeks talked much about literature and especially about English poetry. Solomos next day reciprocated the visit, in the town, and found the opportunity to recite his Italian "Ode for the First Mass" for Trikoupis. The latter then commented: "Your poetic genius will secure for you a good position in the Italian Parnassus. But the first positions there are already taken. The Greek Parnassus has yet to have its Dante." [17]

Trikoupis then explained details about modern Greek literature, and he must have made Solomos realize the need of the Greek nation, now fighting for freedom, to have its own Bard and to prove itself a worthy descendant of the ancient Greeks. The idea was noble, but Solomos had reservations about his Greek. Trikoupis then volunteered to tutor him in the language and offered him a crash course using the *Lyrics* (1811) of Athanasios Christopoulos as a textbook.[18] Solomos's progress with Trikoupis must have been rapid and satisfactory. After all, Dionysios was not learning a foreign language, but improving his own mother tongue which, until then, he had used only orally and on limited occasions. With books, poems, songs, the *Romaic Language* (1814) of John Vilaras, and a number of other texts, Solomos began gradually to acquire the desired degree of mastery and to feel more and more confident with his modern Greek. That was not an easy task, for as George Seferis has observed, Solomos and Andreas Kalvos were always hindered by the lack of a written literary language capable of expressing refined and subtle meanings.[19] It is not an exaggeration to state that Solomos forged the modern Greek literary language virtually from scratch.

IV *The Patriotic Works*

The ten years of Dionysios's life on Zakynthos (1818–28), were the most productive ones in terms of quantity. The quality of his verse kept improving steadily from year to year, sometimes even from poem to poem. Solomos was constantly striving for the ideal poetic expression in the ideal artistic form. He was one of the most protean and dynamic of all Greek poets.

Under the inspiration of the progress of the revolution in Greece, his liberal training and disposition, and a number of literary sources and echoes, Solomos composed the one hundred and fifty-eight quatrains of his "Hymn to Liberty," in May, 1823.[20] This long poem was a tour de force for the twenty-five-year-old intellectual who, only a few months before, was wondering if he knew enough Greek.

"The Hymn" was an immediate success, not only as a beautiful composition, but also as an impressive document dramatically proclaiming the holy rights of the people of Greece to freedom and dignity. The poem was copied and circulated widely in the Greek and philhellenic circles outside Greece and was invariably received with enthusiasm.[21] A manuscript was sent to John Murray, of all publishers, in London, and probably another to Goethe for his reaction.[22] Nothing is known about the fate of these two. But a third one, sent to Claude Fauriel, was put to good use. Fauriel published it in his celebrated collection of Greek folk songs in Paris (1825) along with a prose translation in French, as he also did with Reghas Pheraios's "War Song."[23] Charles Brinsley Sheridan translated the whole collection into English verse and had it published in London the same year.[24] Thus, Solomos's first great poem began to receive the attention it deserved. At the same time, the cause of Greek independence was served by Dionysios Solomos in the best possible manner. For it was now possible for all these Romantic philhellenes who had been lamenting the "Glory that was Greece," as Byron had done in *Childe Harold, Don Juan, The Giaour, The Siege of Corinth,* and other works, to realize that Greece was very much alive and needed their moral and material support to secure a place under the sun.

In 1825 the "Hymn to Liberty" was published at Missolonghi, along with a good prose Italian translation by the poet's friend, Gaetano Grassetti. Missolonghi, which was known to the world as the Greek town where Lord Byron died in 1824, had withstood a savage Turkish siege. Two years later a second siege by a combined Egyptian and Turkish crack force under Ibrahim Pasha resulted in a heroic *exodus* (sally) of most of the surviving population and in the almost total destruction of the legendary town and its heroic defenders.[25] But Solomos was to connect his name more than once to the living legend of Missolonghi, for his greatest poem, "The Free Besieged," and "The Woman of Zakynthos"—the powerful prose draft of a satire—were inspired by the tragedy of its people.

Lord Byron's death offered Solomos the opportunity to compose an appropriately long tribute, the "Lyrical Poem on the Death of Lord Byron," in 1824. Its form and technique do not differ substantially from those of the "Hymn to Liberty," nor is its idiom smoother or considerably improved. However, it served its purpose well, as Solomos took it upon himself to express the gratitude of his nation to this famous philhellene. Andreas Kalvos also composed at that time an ode as a tribute to Byron, "The Britannic Muse." Their example inspired Achilleus Paraschos, Angelica Palli, and Miltiades Malakasis, among other poets of the generations that followed.[26]

The events of the Greek Revolution were to provide inspiration for two more poems of this period, the celebrated epigram, "To Psara" (1824–25), and the ode "To Markos Botsaris," the Suliot commander who fell fighting heroically in 1823. Another dramatic episode, the suicide of an innocent young lady because of slanderous gossip, inspired Solomos to write the beautiful "Poisoned Girl," in 1826.

The idea of a long Romantic poem of epic dimensions—like those of Monti, Manzoni, Byron, Shelley, and others—had always excited the imagination of Solomos. True to his role as the Bard of his Nation the young poet wanted to conceive of a Greek story, in which reality and imagination would cooperate in creating its plot and characters, and his intellect could control the sentimental side and provide the necessary ethical message.

Some early lyrics could be incorporated into this ambitious composition, and stanza forms and meters popular in Europe could now become nationalized Greek. Solomos knew that other Greeks before him had written in *ottava rima* and other Italianate verse forms and meters. His, however, would be a work comparable to those of Byron, Tasso, or any other great contemporary "classic" poet. Thus "Lambros" was launched, and the fragments which make it up occupied him for over ten years.

The siege and fall of Missolonghi diverted Solomos from other occupations, and the poet began to experiment with the composition of another long poem, one about the heroes of Missolonghi, "The Duty," which later on was to be recast in two entirely different meters and forms as the profound "Free Besieged." Another work was "The Woman of Zakynthos," a subtle blend of patriotism and satire revealing the strange and bitter feelings that governed Solomos's soul often during the years of its composition (1826–29).[27]

To this decade also belong Solomos's satires of Dr. Roidis: "The Medical Council," "The First of the Year" (1824), and "The Scaffolds," in Greek, and several others, including parodies, in Italian. "The Dream" (1826), satirizes the vulgar and corrupt John Martinengo. The years 1818–22 must also have been the period Solomos worked on most of his verse translations into Greek. From linguistic evidence and the versification technique in general, it is not difficult to conclude that the parts of Metastasio's "Spring," "Summer," and other poetic passages, as well as "Desdemona's Song" from *Othello,* and an ode of Petrarch, were rendered in competent Greek verse before Solomos wrote any original Greek works. The useful habit of verse translation, which he had acquired in Italy, was now put to serious use. And these versions were anything but a poor start.

Prior to the excellent prose of "The Woman of Zakynthos," Solomos had composed the "Dialogue," a prose essay in the then popular form of dialogue, which will occupy us later. The deaths of his young friend Spyridon Griparis (December, 1820) and of the much-admired Ugo Foscolo (1827) offered Dionysios the opportunity to compose two funeral eulogies, whose eloquent and properly elevated Italian prose might be an indication of why Solomos had won a rhetoric prize as a student. The scholarly references and critical insights in Solomos's tribute to Foscolo are not negligible, either. In all these prose "essays" Solomos exhibited the other side of his intellectual activity: the theoretician and critic of language and literature.

After the wide publication of the "Hymn to Liberty" and the dissemination of the "Lyrical Poem on the Death of Lord Byron" and the other popular poems and songs of the Zantiot period, the character of the young poet began to show signs of strain caused by fame and all manner of psychological and other pressures. It is known, for instance, that Dionysios became the comic hero of an episode with Demetrios, on a ridiculous argument stemming from their cohabitation in the same family mansion *(domenicale).*[28] A person of quiet disposition and solitary nature since childhood, Dionysios would easily lose his temper. Loud noises bothered him excessively, and life in town became intolerable. Eventually, the need for a change of atmosphere became evident.

CHAPTER 3

Life in Corfu

I A Few Happy Years, 1828–1833

SOLOMOS OCCUPIED a few rooms in a good and quiet neighborhood in Kerkyra and settled down to a simple life of solitude, study, composition, and relaxation, far from the din of the center. The phrase, "There is no doubt that one can live well only alone," found in one of his letters to George Markoras (April, 1831),[1] in addition to other evidence, makes it clear that the first years of Dionysios's life in Corfu were happy ones. Indeed his sojourn there had started under the best of omens.

When the ship bringing Solomos docked in the harbor, in December, 1828, his fame had already preceded him. The faculty of the Ionian Academy, headed by Professor Neophytos Vamvas, paid him a visit of welcome, and Vamvas reminded Solomos that he had sung of Greece's war and that he should now visit her hallowed grounds.[2] Solomos thanked them and politely refrained from accepting the invitation for he preferred to retain his idealized impression of Greece, for the time being.

The political situation, however, had now changed considerably. The Allied fleets of England, France, and Russia had destroyed the combined Turkish, Egyptian, and Tunisian navies in Navarino (Pylos); in 1827, and a powerful French army under General Maison had stayed in southern Greece to force its evacuation by the Ottomans. England, under Sir George Canning, was clearly pro-Greece, and the lord high commissioner of the Heptanese, Sir Frederick Adam—who was married to a Corfiot lady—took a pro-Greek position and gave more power and privileges to the local nobility.[3] Solomos could now focus all his attention on the improvement of his art and on the expansion of his erudition and theoretical preparation.

During these happy years Solomos wrote the serene and refined "Funeral Ode," the widely circulated in manuscript form "To a Nun" (1829), and the fragment "To an English Lady." Nor did he neglect projects he had started in Zante. "The Woman of Zakynthos" must have occupied him again before he finally gave it up, in 1829. The ideas for "The Free Besieged" must have taken a more detailed and concrete form, and "Lambros" must have been retouched. In fact, in 1833, a section consisting of sixteen exquisite *ottavas* was prepared and sent for publication in the *Ionian Anthology*. These *ottavas* of "Lambros" made a profound impression on all.[4] And the sensitive Dionysios, thirty-five years old now and in *"mezzo del camin,"* according to his beloved Dante, must have urgently felt the inner need to create art much closer to the ideal than he had achieved thus far.

II   *The Fragmentary Form of His Greatest Works*

It must be mentioned that a certain disquieting pattern in Solomos's creative career began to be discerned: he would leave unfinished most of his major artistic undertakings. The pattern, one may say, was initiated in Italy, when he did not care to complete his degree at the University of Pavia. In this respect he differed completely from the practical and enterprising Demetrios, who made himself a successful and prominent politician, first in Zante, and then in the whole Heptanese. But Demetrios was not an artist.

Dionysios's continual intellectual growth and rapid emotional and artistic maturity made him outgrow his poetic projects before they had been accomplished. He would then begin to work on newer projects, which he considered much more worthwhile and which, temporarily, would demand all his concentration. These, too, would be eventually abandoned, and his creative energies would be channeled to a still newer and more promising work.

Thus, superficially at least, his greatest poetry was left in the state of what might be considered "work in progress." For it is a dramatic monument to his gradual ascent on the slopes of the Greek Parnassus, that he had, paradoxically, never completed as much as one major poem after the age of about forty. In the process, however, some astonishing passages were composed, time and time again, and these suffice to maintain Solomos at the forefront of modern Greek poetry. Many passages and fragments are accomplished poems in themselves and can be—and have been—considered as individual, independent poems in the very condition he left them. Most of the celebrated parts of his major works constitute landmarks in modern Greek verse that have rarely been equalled, let alone surpassed.[5]

All Greek commentators and critics have volunteered a number of explanations as to why Solomos developed this tendency. Reasons vary from psychological and linguistic to social and historical, and a sampling of them should be made here.

Solomos was neither a diligent worker of verse nor a consistent one. As he was a temperamental person, Dionysios experienced sudden enthusiasms which would inspire him temporarily and would fade away before long, leaving a project just begun. The novelist Gregory Xenopoulos, a fellow Zantiot, mentioned Solomos's limited will power, his almost pathological self-doubt, and a lack of patience commensurate with the intellectual dimensions and demands of his artistic targets. Xenopoulos attributed these to the effects of alcoholism, a condition which Solomos developed in his mature years.[6]

Kostes Palamas—a foremost successor to Solomos as poet of the nation and an astute and erudite critic—discerned a kind of dichotomy in the character of the poet. Solomos was now a patient, dedicated, objective, and profound creator; now a quick—tempered, bored, immature man who would not materialize his plans and move past his first experiments with them.[7]

Nicholas Mantzaros referred to the sudden changes in the desires and plans of Solomos and the constant cancelling of work begun.[8] John Apostolakis observed that Solomos was not writing for an audience since he had lost his faith in his contemporaries and was a withdrawn man living with his poetry.[9] The Nobel Prize winner, George Seferis, remarked on the fact that the state of the language that was available to the poet created insurmountable obstacles.[10] Others have also maintained that Solomos's indirect method of composition—usually a first draft in Italian prose, a second one in Greek prose, and a third one in Greek verse which would be reworked time and again—caused the dissipation of the power of his original and spontaneous inspiration.[11]

Tomadakis and others have mentioned the psychological trauma that Solomos experienced during the five years of the infamous trial (1833—38) and its disastrous effects on the mental state of the poet, who became more insecure and obsessed with his quest for perfection.[12]

This quest for esthetic perfection, which strengthened Solomos's critical insights, was mentioned by Polyhymnia Laskaris, among others, as having an adverse impact on his creativity. Something similar after all had happened to Alessandro Manzoni and even to Coleridge.[13]

Solomos's ambition as an artist outweighed his creative ability, maintained Kostas Varnalis, for "his moral, intellectual, and creative power was inferior to his aspiration," and the poet could not finish his creation because he had given it "unnatural inner dimensions."[14] This view was shared by John Vlachoyiannis, more or less, whereas Spyridon Zambelios, a philologist and purist, thought that Solomos's attempt to create a third and "mixed" school, by combining Classicism and Romanticism, "and his desire to achieve a philosophical end *(proprio)*, had wasted his innate lyrical inspiration."[15]

James Polylas made, as always, a very wise observation to the effect that the work that Solomos had already begun, because of his rapid development as a thinker, and an artist, soon became "dated," so to speak, and no longer satisfied his concept of the ideal.[16] The poet then simply abandoned it, to focus his attention (which did not have a long span), and his physical energy (which was not distinguished by considerable stamina), to the realization of a new project which to Solomos now seemed capable of embodying his poetic ideal.

Evidence, or even proof, of this fact can be found in Solomos's answer to the Italian improviser, Giuseppe Regaldi, in 1851, who asked him why he had left "Lambros" unfinished. "'Lambros' will remain a fragment, because the poem as a whole cannot match the sublimity *(hypsos)* of some of its parts," was the poet's comment.[17] Assuming that Solomos maintained a similar attitude toward his other unfinished compositions, we realize that the poet did not care to complete works in progress: rather he cared to make progress in his work. This attitude toward the art of poetry is idealistic, almost unrealistic. Nobody, then or now, expected all of the parts, stanzas, episodes in "Lambros," or "The Free Besieged," or any other lengthy composition, to be of the same high artistic value and ethical sublimity throughout.

If modern Greece were to turn to Dionysios Solomos's work, in order to establish him as her contemporary Bard, what else, in addition to the six hundred and thirty-two lines of his "Hymn to Liberty" and the slightly longer poem to Byron, could she present to support her claim? The unfinished passages, broken fragments and scattered "shreds"—as one Professor had termed them[18]—of his incomplete compositions? Works without a clear beginning, middle, and an appropriate conclusion?

This conclusion would not have posed great difficulties to European critics. Nobody, for instance, would deny Coleridge's greatness if he were to judge him solely on the basis of the six hundred and twenty-five lines of "The Ancient Mariner." Nor would one reject him for not having completed "Kubla Khan"; on the contrary, one must be grateful to Coleridge for having left us this great "fragment." Coleridge's achievement in English poetry, and his career in general, can help one understand much about Solomos's poetic quest. The case of "Christabel," for instance, can contribute considerably to an understanding of Solomos's artistic dilemma.

Part I of "Christabel" is unanimously recognized as truly great, enchanting, and original. Part II is "less original," less great and enchanting, but still very good.[19] It ends, however, abruptly with many details left untold and the story unresolved. Nor does the "Conclusion to Part II" have any apparent relation to the whole composition. This poem is an excellent example of the difficulties that the great Coleridge encountered during its composition. The first part comes almost spontaneously and sounds natural; the second part needs greater effort and comes less naturally and more laboriously; the third (and concluding) one is not even attempted, for the increased labor required for its making would force the poet to resort to a merely mechanical (though technically correct) versification with little of the true breath of poetry. Coleridge knew better than to do just that; apparently, Solomos must have felt and thought along similar lines, when he encountered the same dilemma.

III *Language*

Solomos's dilemma was even greater because, in addition to most of the problems that Coleridge had to face, he had to overcome the language problem. There is no doubt whatsoever that Greek never came to Solomos's lips as naturally and easily as English did to Coleridge's. And the Greek he wanted to use had yet to be enriched with the appropriate vocabulary. This formed a vicious circle, for Solomos loathed the *Katharevousa* (puristic), the language that most scholars used. Though his rejection of the artificial, puristic expression was a sound one artistically, Solomos found himself in a linguistic predicament with virtually "no exit."

Earlier in his poetic career, shortly before and after Trikoupis's visit (1822), Solomos had discovered modern Greek literature and had read and studied the works of the "Cretan school"—the epic *Erotokritos;* the long pastoral "The Shepherdess"; the tragedy *Abraham's Sacrifice,* and others—as well as the Anacreontics, lyrics, and satires of Christopoulos and Vilaras; the patriotic harangues in verse of Martelaos, Reghas, and Thomas Danelakis; the Zantiot poetic tradition we have already mentioned; and of course, the rich tradition of demotic songs from many parts of Greece, including Cyprus. But the thematic range of these works was limited, and the intellectual level of their often charming idioms was desperately inadequate.

Solomos was aware of the organic weaknesses of the vernacular idiom and of the nature of demotic poetry and communal balladry. In a letter to his friend George Tertsetis (June, 1833), Solomos explained the need for the artist to start with the language of the Klephtic songs and, then, to "rise vertically" without stopping there.[20] This is what, for instance, the prolific Valaoritis failed to achieve in his numerous and lengthy poems. Their language and poetic substance seldom surpass the level of the anonymous, unsophisticated folksinger. Palamas was the poet who marvelously succeeded in achieving this—despite his frequent rhetoric—but he had the benefit of a tradition and excellent models, the very works of Solomos.

It is known that Solomos would often approach simple people—peasants and folksingers—trying to hear and master their colloquial Greek.[21] Perhaps even his proverbial love for children, and his generosity to them, were due, in part, to the satisfaction and pleasure he derived from listening to their innocent and charming prattle. In one of his letters to his beloved George de Rossi (c. 1825), one of the two Greek words in it is *revythaki* (small chick-pea), which charmingly describes the little nose of de Rossi's infant daughter.[22] Solomos would not have used this familiar Greek expression in an Italian letter had he not heard it from the mouth of either this or some other child.

Solomos's linguistic preparation from the study of the existing modern Greek texts, and this practical and oral approach to the language, was adequate for the poems he had conceived and, nearly always, completed during the first ten years or so of his career. For the grandiose "Lambros" and the metaphysical "Free Besieged" of the third draft, it was inadequate. His life as a rich aristocrat and the consequent absence of any need to finish a poem, publish it, and thus earn his living are also mentioned as additional reasons why he left his greatest poetry unfinished.[23] Now, Chaucer left his *Canterbury Tales* in fragmentary form, and Spenser did not finish his *Faerie Queene*, nor did Byron his *Don Juan*. But English critics were more generous to them than some Greek critics were to Solomos.

IV *The Right Approach*

There is a measure of truth in most of these arguments. But with the exception of Linos Polites, Apostolakis, and a few others, many commentators were blind to the fact that Solomos was essentially a lyric poet.

Solomos achieved poetic excellence in his short epigrams or epigrammatic lyrics. That genre enabled him to demonstrate his fantastic ability to concentrate so many intense sentiments and profound thoughts in just a few lines, while at the same time, the organic form of the composition was convincingly the proper one. Lyrics like the early epigram "To Psara" and the last "To Francesca Fraser" are fine examples of Solomos's ability to achieve lyric intensity with an astonishing economy of means.

In short compositions like these, the poet did not have to face the burdensome and rather technical—thus frustrating—problem of language. This is clearly shown by the linguistic perfection of Solomos's lyrics, which is a far cry from the vocabulary of his two patriotic poems.

In addition to this "technical" advantage that short poetic forms offered Solomos, it must be emphasized that the nature of his inspiration, his understanding of the function of poetry, and his particular manner of achieving the poetic essence, were all leading away from the forms of epic and mainly narrative verse. Even his two longest completed poems are lyrical in nature, as their titles proclaim.

That is why several critics rightly complained about the unequal artistic quality among the dozens of stanzas of the "Hymn to Liberty" and the "Lyrical Poem on the Death of Lord Byron."[24] Stanzas conveying the essential poetic essence were superior to others which were merely functional—connecting the various parts, or simply describing facts, or worse, offering advice to the audience.

In the case of these two works, Solomos was capable of producing so many lines and stanzas because the motifs of faith, heroism, and suffering, could, in turns, be exploited for the expression of the central idea, which was a praise of freedom and those who fight for it. They are not even historical, in the sense that *The Oath* (1875) by Gerasimos Markoras, and "Samuel" by Aristotle Valaoritis are, as they concentrate, in detail, on one historical event. Despite their considerable length they are lyric poems, like the odes and hymns of Manzoni, Byron, Shelley, and others on similar subjects.

"Lambros" is the only attempt on the part of Solomos to emulate the contemporary poetic fashion—and most notably Byron's—and to compose a long fictional story in the then popular forms. This idea, however, could be materialized only in some of their parts. Even Byron's narratives approach excellence only in some of their parts. What Solomos achieved in "Fragment 25" could not be repeated again and again, not only because of technical difficulties alone, but mainly because the already composed *ottavas* were those that had expressed the most dramatic, most sublime, and most meaningful parts of the projected story. The quintessence of "Lambros" was thus conceived, composed, and even published. The concept of Schiller's *"Erhabene"*[2][5] (sublime) had already been apprehended and materialized, as far as "Lambros" was concerned, in the *ottavas* of its greatest fragment. If Solomos were to complete all projected parts, he would have, of necessity, to utilize his rather limited energies and resources to do minor work. To crank out "filler" passages, connecting lines, descriptive and functional parts which, regardless of their potential success, would be organically inferior to the already finished lines which had captured the "moment of truth," so to speak, and had expressed its highest poetic essence. Artists like Palamas, on the highest level, and Valaoritis, on the mediocre level, could do, and did, what Solomos could not, or would not, do. Thus, their long lyrical epics are finished and complete, whereas Solomos's were left as monumental fragments. But the "broken columns" of Solomos's poetry, and their scattered pieces, often radiate the very essence of pure poetry. In Palamas's impressive lyrical rhetoric a similar radiation is often clouded by the merely ornamental pyrotechnics and the endless recitativo. In Valaoritis's movingly patriotic effusions the sublime is stretched thin, too thin, to cover most of the whole, and the poetic essence is diluted and confused with sheer sentimentality and sensationalism.

With some modifications Polylas's observation, then, is essentially true. Solomos outgrew his work before it was achieved. His failure to finish "Lambros" was repeated in the case of "The Cretan," and since the "poetic moment of truth" was achieved in the fragment with the "Lady-dressed-in-the-Moon," the supernatural experience of the brave islander, which constituted the essence of that work, the poet had to give up the rest.

Artistic sublimity was achieved more than once in "The Free Besieged," in the brilliant poem "Temptation," in the opening passage with the goddess, and in the lines where the heroic besieged transcend the human condition for a brief moment before the redeeming finality of death. And this greatest of all works by Solomos retained the fluid, plastic, forever in-the-process-of-becoming quality of a free and unlimited spirit. Thus content and form, instinctively rather than intentionally on the part of the artist, were mutually and inseparably combined to become an ethereal expression of inner and complete spiritual freedom, much as Schiller had defined it.

CHAPTER 4

Erudition and Poetics

I *Greek and Latin*

SCHILLER'S THEORY of literature and his verse were not the only works that Solomos perused during the latter part of his life. A glimpse of the accumulated list of his reading cannot fail to impress even the most erudite critic; moreover, it helps one to realize what Solomos was doing over the years, when he was not composing verse, or involved, in one way or the other, in public and family affairs.

The sheer bulk of his reading and its range, complexity, and sophistication—and the known fact that he had mastered all that lore and wisdom—explain clearly how months, years, and decades lapsed while Solomos was sitting at his desk, an open book before him, with all his mental faculties concentrated on the meaning of a paragraph or line. For Solomos was a brooding man, a man floating on the oceans of the spirits; not a man of action, like Byron, who dressed as a soldier and rode his horse inspecting his Suliot warriors a few weeks before his death.

In addition to the already mentioned literary and scholarly works by modern Greek authors, Solomos had received a thorough training in the classics—in the Greek and Latin originals as well as in Italian translations.[1] Sometimes his familiarity with a text and several of its translations is quite apparent. Homer's epics are the best example.

An examination of the passage from Book XVIII of *The Iliad* that Solomos translated into Greek, in his later years, reveals that he had Monti's version, as well as the Greek, in front of him when he was working on it. Solomos's interest in Homer reflects that of Manzoni, Foscolo, and Melchior Cesarotti (1730–1808), all of whom liked Homer, and whose translations of Homer and other works were known to the Greek poet.[2]

References and allusions to and even short quotes from the Greek epics have been traced in the verse and prose of Solomos, in both languages, in numerous instances. A list of Homeric lore in Solomos's writings should include the poems "Homer's Shadow," "Ode to Markos Botsaris," "Lyrical Poem on the Death of Lord Byron," "The Two Brothers," "The Eastern War," "Hymn to Liberty" (stanzas 20, 32, 44, 54, 83), the Italian "A Lord Guilford," the notes to the *ottavas* of "Lambros," the "Thoughts" of the Poet and the third draft of "The Free Besieged," the prose "Dialogue," and the Italian "Eulogy to Ugo Foscolo" and a letter to George Markoras (April 5, 1831).

It is also reported that once Solomos was present in the palace of the high commissioner when an Englishman alluded to the wooden horse episode and the trick Odysseus and the Greeks had used to defeat the Trojans. Solomos overheard the derogatory comment and snapped back that the Greeks had done so to defeat the "barbarians."[3] This was not only a manifestation of Greek pride but also an expression of his understanding of Odysseus's character as well.

References to Hesiod's *Theogony* can be found in Solomos's Italian poems "Orfeo" and a sonnet. *Works and Days* inspired "The Nightingale and the Hawk." N. B. Tomadakis observes that Solomos also knew versions of material from Hesiod by La Fontaine and Vilaras and the Italian translations of Soave and G. Leopardi, who had published his *Titanomachia* in 1817.[4]

Sappho's poetry and tragic life had inspired the Italian "Saffo" (1851), though Solomos knew Foscolo's, Leopardi's, and Lamartine's lines on the great poetess.[5] Orpheus was the subject of an Italian sonnet (1847) and two prose drafts.

Solomos's references to the Greek tragedians are also numerous. For instance, Sophocles is repeatedly mentioned in "The Dialogue," and Aeschylus's *Prometheus Bound* in the notes to "The Free Besieged." Euripides's *Alkestis* has been utilized in the conception of the Italian, "The Veiled Lady," though elsewhere Solomos had expressed his disapproval of Euripides's obsession with passion and his "bad" legacy to the artists of posterity. Stanzas 121–124 of the Byron poem allude to Sophocles and to Aeschylus's *Seven Against Thebes*. A note attached to the "Hymn to Liberty" explains a stylistic detail that often appears in choral songs.

A host of Greek lyric poets are mentioned by Solomos in several works: Tyrtaios in the Byron poem and "The Dialogue," Mimnermos in "Brother and Sister," Alkaios in the Byron poem (stanzas 37–38), Pindar in the "Hymn to Liberty" (Stanza 38 and note to Stanza 51).

Plato and Platonic Idealism are often referred to, or echoed, in "The Dialogue" (cf, *Alkibiades*), in the "Eulogy to Ugo Foscolo," in several

Italian lyrics, and in the conception of the female figure in "The Cretan"—Plato's theory of recollection *(anamnesis)* as expressed in *Phaidon* and *Phaidros.*

Solomos's allusions to Greek history are also frequent. King Leonidas and his Three Hundred Spartans, for instance, are invoked with pride in the "Hymn to Liberty." Marathon is mentioned in a letter to a friend on the occasion of a contemporary battle at the same historical site.[6]

Solomos was also attracted by medieval Greek history, as is shown by the fact that he attempted to write a poem on the Byzantine general Nikephoros Vryennios. Through the Greek Church he came to know the works of Byzantine hymnographers, like John Damaskenos and others, as one can see in "Lambros" and in "The Free Besieged."

The Bible (Greek and Vulgate) was also one of Solomos's favorite books. His familiarity with the Old and New Testaments, the Epistles, and especially his appreciation of David's Psalms, are manifested in poems such as "The Cretan," "The Free Besieged," "Lambros," "To a Nun," "The Woman of Zakynthos," "To Markos Botsaris," "Carmen Seculare," the Byron poem, and others—especially his Italian sonnets on religious themes and holy feasts. Stanzas 97 and 98 of the "Hymn to Liberty" show his knowledge of Saint John's *Apocalypse* as well. Nor were the writings of the Fathers of the Church unknown to him. Solomos in his "Thoughts" and elsewhere alluded to Origen, Saint Augustine, and even Spinoza.

Dionysios Solomos was a competent Latinist, too. There are allusions to Virgil and Catullus in "The Dialogue," the "Eulogy to Ugo Foscolo," an Italian sonnet "To a Wedding," and several other instances. In his letters and prose one finds allusions to Cicero, Catullus, and several other authors, as well as historical personalities. It must be mentioned here, however, that Solomos—much as he admired Virgil's verse—believed that the Roman poet had misunderstood various details and was interested in composing a "pathetic narrative,"[7] whereas Homer's poems were the mode of perfection in Classical art for Solomos.

II *Italian, French, English*

Solomos knew well the Italian classics Dante, Boccaccio, Ariosto, Tasso, Metastasio, Alfieri; and his contemporaries Monti, Manzoni, Foscolo, Leopardi, Pindemonte (1753—1828), Parini (1729—99).[8] His works, Italian and Greek, verse and prose, contain proof of his

understanding of their ideas and technique. Allegorical figures such as
Liberty and Glory, and, of course, the more idealized female figures in
"The Free Besieged," "The Cretan," "The Veiled Woman," "The Greek
Mother," and others, seem to have the Dantean aura of Beatrice.
Imagery utilizing light, a kind of heavenly light, is often used in their
pictorial description by Solomos. Even the despicable Woman of
Zakynthos can be said to be depicted in Dantean hellish imagery. Also
The Divine Comedy is echoed, at least, in the "Hymn to Liberty"
(stanzas 5, 10) and in the epigraph to the poem, and in other works.
Dante's views on the vernacular language, in *De Vulgari Eloquentia,*
were also known to Solomos and influenced him to state his own in the
"Dialogue." *La Vita Nuova* and the *Convivio* had been read by him,
too.[9]

Solomos appreciated the critical ideas of Leopardi and the style in
which he expressed them, but objected to his poetry because of its
pessimism.[10] Monti's and Foscolo's ornate, Neoclassical style did not
particularly appeal to Solomos. On the other hand, he was much at ease
with the general spirit of faith, devotion, partriotism, and liberalism
that Manzoni exhibited in his *Sacred Hymns* and his other numerous
works in all genres.

When one examines his versification, Solomos's debt to Italian song
and poetry becomes apparent. From Dante, for example, he learned the
terza rima, which he naturalized into Greek in his "Ode to the Moon."
From Tasso he learned, in all probability, the use of the *ottava rima* in
serious contexts ("Lambros"), and from others, like Ariosto, in satiric
ones (several Italian *ottavas).* This stanza form, however, was known to
Greek poets of the late Renaissance who had used it in love songs,
especially in Cyprus, and Solomos had read such works. Among minor
Italian authors that Solomos had read , one must mention the naturalist
L. Spallanzani, the historian G. Villani, and the dramatist Carlo
Grozzi.[11]

Solomos knew French well and had read many French authors in the
original or in Italian translations. Montesquieu, Mirabeau, Abbe Prevost,
L. Boudon, Fontenelle, Condorcet, Victor Cousin, and others form part
of Solomos's acquaintance with French thinkers. In a note on the "The
Free Besieged" he refers to P. H. Azais; in still another he mentions
Chateaubriand, Lamartine, and Victor Hugo; Racine is alluded to in
"The Dialogue"; Jean Jacques Rousseau's sociopolitical ideas had also
exercised a considerable influence on Solomos. The ideas of D'
Alembert (1717–83) are also echoed in "The Dialogue," as are those of
the Abbé de Condillac (1715–80), and Court de Grebelin.

"The Dialogue" has references to John Locke and Francis Bacon.[12] Milton, Newton, Byron, Moore, Campbell, Rogers, and Lord Holland are mentioned in the "Eulogy to Ugo Foscolo." Shakespeare and several of his plays are referred to in "The Dialogue," and Desdemona's Song was translated into Greek very early by Solomos. Milton and Byron, as well as Thomas Gray, are mentioned, echoed, or even discussed in some stanzas and notes of the "Hymn to Liberty" and the "Lyrical Poem on the Death of Lord Byron." Shelley seems to have influenced Solomos's "Lambros," or even the "Hymn," according to Tomadakis. Laurence Sterne is alluded to in the "Eulogy to Ugo Foscolo," and among other British novelists Daniel Defoe might have attracted him, for Solomos mentions Friday (from *Robinson Crusoe*) in one Italian sonnet.

Edward Young's *Nights,* as well as Ossianic poetry, both very popular with Solomos's Italian contemporaries, should be included in this list, though he must have experienced them through their imitators. Byron and Byronism had impressed Solomos, as well as all Greek poets of the nineteenth century. Solomos answered Byron's remarks about the deplorable condition of the contemporary Greeks (as expressed in "The Isles of Greece" in *Don Juan),* by reminding him that the Greek people were now fighting for freedom and dignity. Several other passages in Solomos's two long patriotic poems undoubtedly echo Byronic lines. "Lambros," at least in part, is superficially Byronic. Solomos, as Tomadakis and Palamas correctly observed, wanted to compose something in the Byronic vein.[13] But the hero, Lambros, is not what Byron would have created. For Byron was not interested in the humanitarian and moral values that had inspired the Greek poet. Nor is his Lambro, in *Don Juan,* his hero; the young Spaniard, is, of course, the Byronic hero in *Don Juan,* where Lambro simply is one of the villains. But Solomos's idiosyncrasy as a creative artist was so different from that of the amoral and adventurous Englishman that the Greek poet misunderstood the nature of the Byronic hero and thought he was only a rebellious and amoral character who eventually recognizes the magnitude of his sins, even if by then he is close to unavoidable death. The spirit that dominates the passages of "Lambros" is profoundly Christian, patriotic, and humanitarian, with no trace whatsoever of the existential courage with which Byron's faithless heroes usually face the abyss.

Some critics tried to add the names of Coleridge, Wordsworth, and even Poe to Solomos's English readings.[14] This is speculation with no evidence to support it. It is true, however, as Peter Vlastos (and

Romilly Jenkins who echoed him) observed, that in "The Cretan" and Coleridge's "The Ancient Mariner," both mariners feel compelled to narrate their strange, supernatural experiences. On the other hand, "The Cretan" is an idealistic, patriotic poem in a typically Greek verse form;[15] whereas Coleridge's great tale is a "lyrical ballad" with an entirely different purpose, despite the two or three moralizing stanzas at its end.

Solomos knew the English language and probably used it a little, later in his life. S. Trikoupis reported that Solomos knew the English poets well, when he visited him (1822), and understood them much better than he, who had studied in England.[16] Solomos, however, never wrote anything in English.

III *German*

In a letter of Nicholas Luntzis to his son, Luntzis wrote, among others,

> [Solomos] loved me with all his heart, when he discovered the spark that glowed in my soul and thought that with his breath he could make it a big flame. Out of gratitude I tried, as best I could, to explain for him the treasures of German Literature that fed my soul. His spirit received the divine thoughts with enthusiasm and gratitude. Much I translated for him from Schiller whose poetic nature springs forth like a virginal source from the depths of his heart. I made him know the power of the proud will in Fichte, the philosophy of poetry in Schelling, the gigantic obscure greatness of Hegel; I translated for him Varnhagen, passages from the profound, sarcastic Menzel, from the famous J. P. Richter whose affected technique I dislike; I initiated him in the superb mysticism of Boehme. Novalis had appealed to him so much that he thought he had found in me a certain resemblance to Ofterdingen, and instead of calling me by my name he preferred to call me Henry....[17]

This impressive list of German authors is not only substantiated by other pieces of evidence but considerably augmented as well. Hermann Luntzis, Nicholas's German-educated brother, had also translated much for Solomos at his urgent request; and probably John Menagias, James Polylas, and others did the same.

Linos Polites published an authoritative list of Solomos's German readings, in Italian translation;[18] and Marinos Sigouros announced the discovery of fourteen manuscript volumes with Italian translations of German material at Vares, Zante, the country villa belonging to

Demetrios Solomos's descendants. Sigouros believes that the total number of volumes was sixty-four, but this cannot be verified.[19] Some of the German philosophers and poets whose works Solomos had certainly perused are the following: Friedrich Schiller (1759–1805), J. G. Fichte (1762–1814), Friedrich Schelling (1775–1854), Wolfgang Menzel (1798–1873), Friedrich Klopstock (1724–1803), G. A. Burger (1747–94), F. L. Stolberg (1748–1821), J. W. Goethe (1749–1832), Friedrich von Matthison (1761–1831), J. G. von Salis–Sewis (1762–1834), Friedrich A. Schlegel (1772–1829), Novalis (1772–1801), L. Tieck (1773–1813), L. Uhland (1783–1862), Th. Korner (1791–1813), G. W. F. Hegel (1770–1831), Immanuel Kant (1724–1804), and others.

A translation of an excerpt from the Hindu epic *Ramayana* by Walmiki and a few poems by the Dane A. G. Oehlenschlager (1779–1850)—Luntzis knew Danish and was married to a Danish lady—completes Polites's list. Sigouros adds to them some secondary works (analyses, thoughts, comments) by or about F. H. Jacobi (1743–1819), J. G. Hamann (1730–88), W. F. Solger (1780–1819), Rachel Varnhagen (1771–1833)—also mentioned in Luntzis's letter— and F. X. von Baader (1765–1841).

Very early in his career Solomos had paraphrased, in competent Greek verse, Goethe's short lyric "Calm" and, much later, Schiller's epigram "Amusia." Schiller's theory, however, especially his *On Naive and Sentimental Poetry* (1795), had helped Solomos considerably in developing his own poetics.

Greek and English critics have discussed at length the profound influence of the German esthetic philosophers, and especially of Schiller, on Solomos.[20] Kostas Varnalis, however, in his book *Solomos without Metaphysics* (1925), provided significant details and incisive observations on this subject.

A careful study of Solomos's "Thoughts," appended to "The Free Besieged," and other esthetic meditations of the poet, reveals that Solomos considered poetry as lying at the absolute sphere of the Spirit, next to religion and philosophy, as Hegel did.[21] From Hegel and Schiller Solomos borrowed the key terms Idea, Sublime *(hypsos)*, and Absolute, which appear in his esthetic philosophizing.[22] In the "Thoughts" Solomos's Idea implies Hegel's Absolute Spirit, and Schiller's Spiritual Freedom. In art this Idea must be manifested as a conflict between man's moral law and adverse forces (material, ethical, spiritual) as well as the instinct of self-preservation or that of happiness.

The free spirit remains invincible, sacrificing life to duty. The Sublime then has been reached.[23]

"Duty" *(To Khreos)* was the title that Solomos had originally intended for his *magnum opus*, "The Free Besieged." In one of the poet's notes we find the axiom, "Enclose Greece (or something else) deeply within you and you will feel all manner of greatness." In one of the "Thoughts" appended to the poem Solomos had written: "Think out deeply and unequivocally (once and for all) the nature of the Idea before you materialize the poem. In it will find flesh and bones the most essential and sublime content of true human nature, Motherland and Faith." These fervently cherished convictions help one understand why the *magnum opus* had to be patriotic and idealistic. And there was no nobler event of that nature than the almost superhuman sufferings and sacrifices of the heroic defenders of Missolonghi. Their experience would be turned into a poem that would not be narrowly patriotic and topically Greek, but universally humane and beautiful. For the Beautiful, according to Hegel, is the esthetic presentation (or realization) of the Absolute Idea.[24] Solomos, throughout his career, had no use for the principle of art for art's sake, which was timidly appearing then. Poetry to Solomos was much too important and sacred to be exclusively left to the service of the Muses. On the contrary, its aim was to contribute to man's moral improvement, and not to exist in abstraction.

Solomos persistently sought the balance of meaning and expression, implied in this poetics, by changing radically the form of the poem three times, and by continually elevating, sublimating, and universalizing its characters and themes. He plowed and replowed, shaped and reshaped almost every single verse in it, trying to make form and content meet his high standards. This practice was, of course, one of the beliefs and ideals of Classical art.[25]

Solomos was aware of the shortcomings of Classicism alone, or Romanticism alone, in achieving the Sublime, or Schiller's "Erhabene." The first could make a poet seek perfection in the outer form (like Monti, Foscolo, and so many Neoclassicists). The other could cause the poet to be carried away by an excessive expression of feeling (like Lamartine) at the expense of form. To avoid the dilemma posed by the easily sentimental and sensational (what Valaoritis could not avoid), and the ornate, rigidly controlled form (Kalvos's weakness) that almost freezes the feelings, Solomos kept reminding himself to try and achieve a "mixed" but "legitimate" genre.[26] It would be an injustice to say that Solomos failed to create this "new genre"; for even in his early works he nearly always succeeded in maintaining an amazing balance between content and form.

In a brief Italian note concerning lyric poetry Solomos candidly wrote:

> Observe the intellectual when he talks. Catch him at one transition he makes from one sentence to the other to reach his goal, and tell him: "Look here, man, you passed through here and went there (things that seem unfitting), and you did so because logic dictated it to you. I will show you now that lyric poetry does the same, and it does nothing else but imitate the logic of some intelligent people in their thoughts; it does nothing else, I say, but imitate them, only making the exterior (outer) expression of their speech bolder."[27]

This reference to logic (reason) is an outgrowth of Solomos's understanding of the nature of poetry. To him poetry was Reason, in the Hegelian sense, translated into images and sensations.[28] He had meant something similar when he compared Milton and Byron and concluded that "The difficulty a writer experiences (I am referring to a great writer) does not lie in the demonstration of imagination and passion, but in the subordination of these two elements, in time and with pain, to the meaning of art."[29]

Solomos achieved this "subordination," actually a balance, with skill even when he wrote about the deaths of heroes, friends, relatives, or even little children. In none of his elegiac pieces—what Tomadakis classified as "Requiems"—is sorrow, or any other sentiment, the dominant characteristic of the poem. Nor, on the other hand, are stanza form and general technique muzzling the poet's feelings. For instance, his poem "To Mr. George de Rossi" exhibits the most delicate handling of the death of a beloved person, a theme that many other Romantic poets would have turned into a source of tears and despair.

Solomos's adherence to his idealistic poetics, with its very high, almost unattainable standards, had, naturally, an adverse effect on his poetic output. He sacrificed quantity to high quality. Though Solomos missed the opportunity to complete poetic monuments worthy of a great artist, he achieved repeatedly what we have termed "the poetic essence." For above all classifications, the only one he personally strove to achieve is, undoubtedly, the poet of "essence."

CHAPTER 5

The Trial and the End

I *Human Malice*

JOHN, THE FIRST SON of Emmanuel and Angelica Leontarakis, was offered the opportunity to advance socially, as his half-brother Dionysios generously contributed toward the expenses of his education in Italy (1824–33). John Leontarakis, there is no doubt, had a good time in Italy, drinking, gambling, wenching, and, occasionally, studying at Bologna and Pisa. He succeeded, however, in earning his law degree, though Dionysios, who had been kept posted of his escapades, never believed it. Upon his return to Zante, through Corfu, in October, 1833, John used the name John Leontarakis–Solomos at the authorities of both ports. While in Corfu he even attempted to talk to Solomos, when he was taking his constitutional at the Esplanade. Angry at his half-brother for his bold usurpation of the Solomos's surname, which he took as a sign of ingratitude, the austere Dionysios ignored John. The latter then assumed an air of importance and moved away.[1]

Dionysios then instructed Demetrios and the family lawyer and friend, John Galvanis, to have the Leontarakis family evicted from the Solomos house in the town of Zante. "Tell them I want the house for myself," he writes angrily to Galvanis.[2] The temperamental artist, full of indignation, hurt in his pride, wanted to hurt back. "Prince John," as Solomos called him, made things worse, for he sued Dionysios and Demetrios Solomos, claiming that he was the only legitimate son of Count Nicholas, born within the three hundred days after his father's death. Italian law recognized such a child as "posthumous legitimate son."[3] If the court were to recognize this claim, John would receive a substantial part of the family estate and the title. Since, however, by then Robert Solomos had died, John would have emerged as the only legitimate Count Solomos.

One can imagine the feelings of Solomos. John he had helped financially; Angelica and Emmanuel he had provided with a home to live; and this was how they repaid him. Trying to usurp his property was perhaps less audacious than the Leontarakis's endeavor to present their illegitimate son as legitimate at the expense of Dionysios, a man who had only helped them. Dionysios, however, in another letter (November, 1833), asked Galvanis to help Angelica financially on his behalf, without letting anyone know.[4] He also asked about the condition of Emmanuel and his children. There is no hatred nor any unjustifiable wrath in these letters. Dionysios was more afflicted with human weakness than just angry. He even asked Demetrios not to disclose John's petty thefts to Galvanis, feeling perhaps that the lawyer might use this information in court.[5]

The two brothers won the trial, but John appealed the verdict, only to lose again. Never giving up, he took the case to the Supreme Court, where he lost irrevocably. By then it was 1838.

This five-year period was a critical one for Dionysios, as it would have been for any human being exposed to such a humiliating and scandalous experience. No critic has failed to mention the adverse effect that the course of the trial, and its implications, must have had on the sensitive poet. With his inner world in turmoil, and the outside world about to collapse, Solomos would have been a superman had he been able to continue producing idealistic verse during that fatal period or soon after it.

Dissatisfied with composition that came to him easily, Solomos sought profundity of meaning and perfection of form, with an ever increased urgency. Philosophy was now the target of his mental activities, and it, in addition to religious faith, must have helped an embittered and unhappy Solomos face the problem of his existence as a man and as an artist.

Emotions generated by this unhappy event, however, found vent in verse as well. Dionysios, soon after the trouble had started, in 1833, went to Zakynthos probably to coordinate his actions with those of Demetrios. There he remembered the slandered young lady who had committed suicide and the moving poem, "The Poisoned Girl," he had written in 1826 defending her honor. As if to do something to express his own emotions, now that he considered himself also a victim of human baseness, he wrote "The Poisoned Girl in Hades," the same year. This poem shows Solomos's changing, and improving, attitude as a poet. He does not try to be didactic and moralistic now. His love for the ideal is implied, as is his resentment toward prosaic reality and human weakness. Though most critics believe that in that poem Solomos somehow identifies with the innocent and savagely slandered girl, "The Poisoned Girl in Hades" could give vent only to noble feelings. To castigate the base and ungrateful Leontarakis, Solomos composed a long satire, "The Hair," in 1833.

Solomos visited Zante for the last time in 1836. This was his third trip there, the two others had taken place in 1831 and 1833.[6] Upon his return to Kerkyra, far from the relatives and situations of Zakynthos, Dionysios settled into a life of increased solitude and isolation. By 1838 all memories from his life in Zante seem to have become part of a distant and better-to-be-forgotten past.[7] His mother, who had been the object of his adulation through 1833, should be forgotten too. The drinking of wine, which had always been one of Solomos's little pleasures, becomes now a habit, a necessity, an addiction.

II *Skepticism*

The fact that Solomos became an increasingly shy and retiring man does not imply that he had become some sort of a misanthrope as well. For Solomos was never unresponsive to spontaneous shows of recognition and respect.

In 1833 King Othon of Greece sailed by the island, and Solomos's patriotic feeling made him attempt a poem commemorating the event. But the times were not propitious, and the lines "On Crete" were abandoned. In 1850 another visit of the king inspired the epigram "To the King of Greece." Solomos never lost his interest in Hellenism, but the sad state of affairs in postrevolutionary Greece made him lose any desire he might have had to visit her. In letters to trusted friends, like Judge Tersetis, the poet made it clear that this was not the Greece he had idealized in his innocent imagination.[8] Indeed, contemporary Greece was plagued by all the problems that an emerging state often faces: poverty and squalor, limited educational opportunities, financial ruination, petty selfishness, widespread dissatisfaction among the warriors who had liberated it, even anarchy. The first governor, Count Capo d'Istria, was murdered in 1832. Othon, the inexperienced but well-meaning Bavarian prince who succeeded him when Greece became a kingdom, failed to inspire lasting enthusiasm and affection in his war-torn and rebellious nation. Nor was he properly assisted by the highhanded German autocrats who acted as advisers and manned most governmental posts in the early phase of his administration.

Most biographers agree that Solomos, in his later years, had lost his youthful liberalism and enthusiasm.[9] This is natural in most aging people, especially those who have suffered and have seen many of their dreams evaporate. A withdrawn and contemplative man, like Solomos, had no reason to continue the image of the eager, patriotic liberal and moral reformer. Liberty was in bad shape in poorly run and almost anarchic Greece. New masters had simply replaced the Turks. Back home, things under the British were far from ideal, but the British domination would not suffer in a comparison with the administration of free Greece. Thus Solomos did not show any interest in patriotic agitators, whose aim was the union *(enosis)* of the Seven Islands with Greece. This attitude of Solomos has often been criticized as pro-British, conservative, and even unpatriotic. It should not be forgotten, however, that regardless of any personal disposition Solomos once more felt that he was not at liberty to take sides in that controversial issue. His brother Demetrios had always been on excellent terms with the British. He had married early and had a family now. Also he had a successful political career, and after having served as eparch (chief executive) in Zakynthos, he became president of the Ionian Senate in 1850. As Jenkins reports, the British even knighted Demetrios for his meritorious services to the Ionian state.[10]

Twelve years after the notorious trial, another calamity shattered the calm of the Solomos family. Demetrios's second daughter, Angelica, whose godfather was Dionysios, committed suicide, at the age of twenty-four, on the eve of her wedding. The shock was tremendous, and the two aging brothers, who had been very close since the beginning of the trial, felt more strongly than ever before their emotional dependence on one another. Letters of Solomos to his brother, at that period, make moving reading as the poet tries to console Demetrios on the loss of the idealistic girl. "Thousands of people should have learned from her how to live and how to die," Dionysios writes, admiring Angelica for preferring death over a man she did not love.[11] One readily infers from these facts that Dionysios could not have wished to create additional trouble for his afflicted brother.

III *Love and Friendship*

One of the major mysteries in Solomos's life is his love affairs, if there were any. Imaginative biographers tried to find evidence or sentimental involvement in some of his lyrics. Even the heroine of the charming song, "The Little Blonde Girl," was considered a youthful love of the poet. Today, though, we know that the song was based on a real episode—the departure of a beautiful refugee girl from Chios. Solomos, who was always fascinated by the innocence and beauty of children, immortalized the child's departure for Europe.

Because of the complete lack of information related to Solomos's love life or sexual habits, speculation about possible escapades, abnormalities, or asceticism has been substituted, only making an unclear issue even more vague. One may assume that Solomos had solved this problem in a practical way, as so many aristocrats had done clandestinely. His relocation to Corfu could have helped in this respect, too.

A beautiful Italian prose draft of a poem, "The Veiled Lady," may offer a hint about a possible love affair, a platonic one to be sure, of Solomos's. According to Phanes Michalopoulos, Dionysios had fallen in love with Adelaide Karvela while in Zante. Adelaide, however, married the Italian scholar Gaetano Grassetti and settled in Corfu (1828). Solomos and Grassetti were friends. Grassetti had translated Solomos's "Hymn" for the Missolonghi edition (1825). While in Corfu, Solomos could visit the Grassettis and thus satisfy his platonic feeling for beautiful Adelaide.[12] She died in middle age, in 1846, and Solomos, then in his late forties, was probably inspired to compose a poem about her divine form, obliquely confessing his love. If this hypothesis is sound, the mystery is almost solved. Knowing how Solomos idealized women in real life (his mother, his niece Angelica, several British ladies) and in his verse, we can assume that he remained faithful to one woman—the Ideal One—for his whole life.

His idealistic attitude toward women is also manifested in his letters to his trusted friend and lawyer, John Galvanis, during the years of the trial. Galvanis was contemplating marriage and had asked Solomos for his opinion. The poet, bitterly disillusioned with society, cautioned the lawyer to avoid committing himself to a girl whose real character he had no way of knowing. Steeped in the Venetian tradition, Solomos was afraid of the "angelic creatures," the pure maidens, who, soon after the ceremony, developed into earthly females, domineering and demanding.

These letters are concrete evidence, however, of how Solomos felt about marriage.[13] The friction that the wives of Demetrios and Robert might have caused among the Solomos brothers—if the rumors are true[14]—were another possible source of apprehension which contributed to Dionysios's obsession against marriage and which led to his celibacy. We know, however, that by the time of the trial these petty differences were settled and that the poet had developed warm feelings for his brothers' families, his nieces and nephews.

Solomos made a number of good friends during the last decades of his life, and he experienced the maturity and spiritual satisfaction that great and lasting friendships offer on a mutual basis.

The composer Nicholas Mantzaros (1795–1875) had been one of his closest friends and collaborators since 1828. Mantzaros is the artist who composed moving melodies for Solomos's "Hymn to Liberty," the Byron poem, and several lyrics.[15] His house, which Solomos visited often, was frequented by writers, scholars, and artists, such as John Zambelios (1787–1854), Andreas Mustoxydis, Peter Vrailas–Armenis, and the Italians Niccolo Tommaseo (1802–74) and Giuseppe Regaldi (1809–83). Most of these men have left us valuable written accounts of the character of the poet and the impact of his works.

This group was increased around 1838 by the arrival from Germany, where they had gone to study, of Spyridon Zambelios (1813–81), Hermann Luntzis (1806–68), and John Menagias. These men became the transmitters of German literature, philosophy, and lore, and provided the opportunity for further intellectual development for Solomos in the same way the youthful friends in Zante had done in the period 1818–28.[16]

The most meaningful of these friendships was, undoubtedly, that of James Polylas (1825–96), whom Solomos must have met around 1842.[17] Polylas, who combined scholarship with creative imagination, is the man who understood the poet and his works better than anyone else. His "Prologue" to the first and posthumous edition of Solomos's works (1859) is a monument to modern Greek scholarship (which then began to develop) and to the artist he admired and understood.

Other Greek friends of that period were Julius Typaldos (1814–81), a poet and disciple; Andreas Laskaratos (1811–1901), the famous Cephalonian satirist; Gerasimos Markoras (1824–1811), son of George and a poet, too; Peter Quartano, co-editor of the first edition of Solomos's works; and several others.[18]

During his 1836 trip to Zante, Solomos met the Polish poet Julius Slowacki (1809–49), who also wrote about him, and commented, with some dose of irony, on Solomos's aristocratic pose, feeling of self-importance, and the fact that after the great success of the "Hymn to Liberty," Solomos "by now burns and destroys whatever he writes."[19]

This comment of Slowacki did not come as a surprise, though. When Polylas and Quartano published Solomos's *Found Remains,* the eager and anxious Greek public was profoundly disappointed by the number and shape of the verse it contained. Rumors then began to rise: some Solomos manuscripts had been stolen, destroyed (by the poet himself or his heirs), lost, or suppressed by relatives.[20] Though there may be some degree of truth in these willful or innocent speculations, it is impossible to accept that Solomos had actually completed all of "The Free Besieged," or "Lambros," and other poems, and later on, made an "auto da fe" out of them. Nor does the condition of the found remains, the work in progress, suggest that the poet was anywhere near the end of his ambitious projects. Nor would he destroy papers containing a completed poem, when he zealously kept in his trunk papers with the outline or unfinished draft of the same poem.

There are, however, categorical assertions by honest and trustworthy witnesses which strengthen these speculations. Mantzaros maintained, for instance, that he had seen a copybook of a certain color wherein Solomos had copied some of his verse.[21] That particular manuscript has never been found. Polylas also mentions that Solomos "had completed 'Porphyras' and was thinking of publishing it." Moreover, the poet intended to commit to print simultaneously "a part of 'The Free Besieged.'"[22]

Now, there is a great deal of difference between Mantzaros's statement and that of Polylas. "Porphyras" in *almost* complete. At a felicitous moment Solomos might have composed (even orally) the few connecting and concluding lines that are missing and might have recited them to a friend. In that sense Polylas may be right. Similarly, the "Temptation," part of Solomos's *magnum opus* is a quite finished poem itself. But the loss of a whole notebook leaves the reader wondering whether he has missed a major poem (or poems) that has not survived elsewhere in its definitive and perhaps, publishable, form.

During the period 1849–55 Solomos made the acquaintance of the Dalmatian scholar Tommaseo, who also knew Manzoni and Mustoxydis. Tommaseo, who married a Greek widow, knew Greek, and worked diligently to propagate Greek vernacular literature. The poet was also very polite to the Dalmatian's plebeian wife, and Tommaseo was moved by his humanism. In an international folk-song anthology he edited in 1842, Tommaseo was assisted by the poet, and included his lyric, "The Death of the Shepherd," in the third (and Greek) volume.[23] According to Polylas, Tommaseo, who was critical of Solomos's unwillingness to finish his works, had commented that the Germans gave common things the aspects of profundity, whereas Solomos could make profound meanings sound simple. Tommaseo also recorded an interesting episode of the year 1853. An Italian refugee had quarreled with a Greek over religious differences and had killed him. The Greek populace rose up in fury and demanded the death penalty for the culprit. Solomos then courageously intervened and appealed for clemency, despite the opposition of the excited Corfiots.[24]

An equally prolific writer and colorful man was Regaldi. A successful improviser in verse and public lecturer, Regaldi met Solomos in Corfu in 1851 and saw him often until his departure in 1853. The two poets spent long hours discussing topics of common interest, and the Italian recorded his impressions in a study of Solomos. "When one listened to him for the first time," wrote Regaldi, "he thought that long passages of his speech were academic pages prepared with good care, rather than creations of a spontaneous speech on the spur of the moment." Regaldi commented on Solomos's character as well and found him "polite and refined in his manners, clear conversationalist and open—hearted." He added, however, that Solomos "was a continuous revelation of the harmonies of love and faith," only to those few he allowed to become familiar with him.[25]

From the company he kept one easily infers that Solomos cared to meet only men and women of high spiritual caliber, idealists and humanists believing in the moral principles of the Greco-Christian civilization and Western tradition in general. In this respect, Solomos could not remain indifferent to Englishmen, who exhibited these worthy qualities, even if they were, technically, the conquerors of his country.

After the pro-Greek change in British policy (1825), a slow and gradual softening of position occurred in Solomos's heart. England was no longer the greedy and cynical power he depicted in his youthful "Hymn to Liberty," in the "Lyrical Poem on the Death of Lord Byron," and elsewhere. England was now one of the protectors of the free, but small and weak, Greece that she had helped to liberate.

Mutual and genuine feelings of friendship and affection must have inspired Solomos to compose Italian and Greek lyrics, mostly epigrams, honoring British friends. "To Francesca Fraser" (1849) is one of his greatest; and the Italian "Ad Alice Ward" (1853–54) and "Al . . . Giovanni Fraser" (1855) are indicative of Solomos's feelings for Sir John Fraser, the secretary of the government. Fraser kindly reciprocated by composing an epigram to Solomos in Classical Greek before he left Corfu.[26] Solomos was on good terms with most of the high commissioners who succeeded the hated Maitland. Sir Henry George Ward often invited him to the palace, and the Greek count would invariably oblige. This should not make one assume that Solomos was an angelic man, always considerate and never unwise. On the contrary, occasionally, and usually over minor arguments, Solomos's temper would flare, and he would make unpleasant remarks about devout friends or openly quarrel with them. In most cases, however, his bad temper would subside in time, and he would become friendly and considerate again to the Greeks, Italians, and Englishmen he befriended. With Lord Ward he had at least one such major misunderstanding, but Ward's belated diplomacy, and his fascinating daughter's charm, eventually won back the proud and stubborn Greek artist.[27]

During the last decade of his life Solomos felt unusually close to his brother. Much of their correspondence in that period deals with the persons who were involved in the political affairs of the state and needed Demetrios's help or could offer him their help.[28] His influence with the British was considerable. It is known, for instance, that Dionysios secured a position for his friend Quartano at the public library, though the English official in charge wanted to appoint someone else.[29]

It seems that Solomos gave up the idea of completing "The Free Besieged" around 1849. The same year King Othon awarded him Greece's highest order in recognition of Solomos's contribution to the cause of Greek independence.[30] Mantzaros had been similarly honored in 1845. Solomos made several more attempts to compose, in Greek or in Italian, poems of high quality, and though he rarely finished them, it was evident that he was capable of arresting the moment of truth, of catching and expressing the poetic essence. Time, however, was not as readily at his disposal as before. "The Porphyras" (1847–49); "Nikephoros Vryennios," a barely begun passage; "The Eastern War" (c. 1854); "To the Death of His Niece" (1850); "To the King of Greece" (1850); and "Carmen Seculare" seem to be Solomos's last Greek verse. Only the epigrams to King Othon and Miss Fraser were completed.

The international company the poet was keeping then, and the Italian language they used, probably made him try to achieve the Schillerian "Erhabene" in Italian as well. Solomos's earlier Italian compositions were mostly improvisations, which, despite their correct versification, honesty of feeling, and mastery of form, cannot be considered as equally good as his Greek poems, let alone great verse. In the period 1847–51, Solomos worked on several Italian projects.

When a friend mildly objected to the hero and subject matter of "Porphyras," a British soldier, which in the critic's opinion was hardly a Greek topic, the poet promptly retorted, "The Nation must learn to consider National whatever is True." [31] This answer is indicative of Solomos's humanism, and his transcendence of the narrowly topical and temporal in his quest for the poetic essence. Nor is this comment different in spirit to Keats's proverbial utterance, " 'Beauty is truth, truth is beauty,'–that is all/ Ye know on earth, and all ye need to know." [32]

The original sonnet "Orfeo" (1847) and its versions, "Saffo" and its variations, "La Navicella Greca" (The Little Greek Ship), written in 1851 and almost completed, and the sonnet to Stelios Markoras's death (1852) stand out among the rest of Solomos's late Italian poems. A group of compositions just begun but not substantially worked out includes "L'Albero Mistico"–a kind of equivalent to the Greek "Carmen Seculare"–"L'Avvelenata," "Il Giovane Guerriero," and an untitled fragment.

Ironically, most profounder ideas and, generally speaking, subject matter of appropriate magnitude (in the Aristotelian sense), are found in Italian prose outlines of never "born" poems. "La Madre Greca," "La Donna Velata," and "L'Usignolo e lo Sparviere," plus newer plans for another "Orfeo," would undoubtedly have achieved artistic sublimity even in a fragmentary form. These poems or outlines, though written in Italian, are Greek in spirit and color. There is no doubt that some were meant to be turned into Greek poetry, later on, for an exquisite Greek verse was found in the manuscript of "The Greek Mother." Solomos was nearly always obsessed with a certain idea, and he would strive to give it appropriate poetic form and utterance in several poems, sometimes in both languages. This characteristic attitude of artistic commitment, profundity, and poetic integrity, had been misunderstood by some poor critics who had complained that Solomos repeated himself frequently.[33] But hadn't Homer, or any other major writer and artist, done the same?

As Solomos advanced in years his health deteriorated, and he was often plagued by various ailments. He was now getting obese, and his nerves and emotions were often strained. By 1850 his works were popular all over Greece, but one of his finest triumphs was his recitation of "La Navicella Greca," on August 20, 1851, before an elite audience packed in at the splendid hall of the Ionian Academy.[34] Greeks, Italians, and British were elated and applauded Solomos with enthusiasm. When he was making his way down the steps of the Academy, the honor guards presented arms, the audience was still loudly applauding. Solomos, that evening, must have crossed the great Esplanade, his favorite walk, with a feeling of self-satisfaction and accomplishment.

As was mentioned earlier, the elderly poet continued working at his verse, now in Greek, then in Italian. He suffered one cerebral stroke, soon after the triumph at the Academy.[35] He managed, however, to recover from it and return to his papers and normal activities. Demetrios, dejected and broken because of Angelica's suicide and other blows, resigned his high position and returned to their birthplace, Zakynthos, in 1852. Dionysios stayed on in Kerkyra, also dejected and often bedridden, but at times experiencing hours of serene happiness and great mental clarity. He kept seeing friends, eating and drinking well, dressing in an impeccable manner, and taking his constitutionals at the spacious Esplanade. He was now a renowned, admired, and loved personality, greeted with respect by all who chanced to meet him.

Solomos would often experience sudden fits of melancholy, even when he was in enjoyable company. At one of his last parties he told his companions, "I am going to leave you soon." [36] The last and fatal stroke came on February 21, 1857, three months after the third one, which had kept him in bed since November, 1856.[37]

It is said that while on his deathbed the poet remembered his beloved tutor, Santo Rossi, with gratitude, and that he recited Stanza 95 of his "Hymn to Liberty," which describes the allegory of Liberty in imagery of light:[38]

> Fiery gleams, a flashing cluster,
> Hang from lip, eye, forehead bright,
> Hand and foot are clothed in luster,
> And around you all is light.[39]

The sad news of his death spread rapidly over Kerkyra. The Ionian Senate suspended its session and declared a period of public mourning. The lord high commissioner, Sir John Young, and all his civic and military officers attended the magnificent public funeral, as did bishops and clergymen, the consul of Greece and other dignitaries, as well as thousands of simple peasants and citizenry from all over Corfu.[40] It was the year that saw the publication of Baudelaire's *The Flowers of Evil.* Two years later, Palamas, the future National Poet, was born.

CHAPTER 6

Solomos's Apprenticeship

I *The Early Italian Verse*

WHEN DIONYSIOS wrote his long poem "The Destruction of Jerusalem" (La Distruzione di Gerusalemme), in Cremona, about 1815, he was only seventeen. Although he composed 259 lines under the subtitle "First Canto," Solomos abandoned this exercise in *terza rima* when he apparently realized that he could turn out competent rhymes. The theme of the canto he completed, however, was the biblical prophecy of the destruction of this city.

The poem opens with a description of the Crucifixion of Christ and the crowds of people gathering to watch the event.[1] A venerable old priest feels profound sorrow, but the Jews have become so corrupt that nobody shares his grief. A group of abandoned Virtues roam outside the walls of the sinful city, unheeded by the populace who embrace the various personified Vices. Several stanzas are allocated to the allegorical depiction of Ignorance, Cruelty, Sloth, Intemperance, Impiety, and the other various Sins. The pious priest preaches repentance and a return to righteousness, but the thunderous response of the mob is, "Death to the Nazarene." The elements are then described as experiencing profound dejection and sorrow because of Jesus' sufferings. Christ himself is then seen coming, bearing his own cross, and his distraught mother tries to get close to him. When Christ dies, all nature goes into convulsions, and a prophetic voice is heard,

Yes, Jerusalem, you will fall; I already see you
Swimming into your own blood, and through the slaughtering swords
I see you lifting your sight toward the sky.
But the stern sky smiles at your horror.

Little is original in this poetic exercise. Dante's verse has offered the stanza form, much of the imagery, and much of the technique of allegorical abstractions. Tasso's *Jerusalem Delivered* may possibly have suggested the title and, perhaps, the epic genre with divisions into cantos. Manzoni's fervent Christian faith and adherence to moral principles undoubtedly inspired the general atmosphere and tone of Solomos's poem. But the exquisite treatment of nature, which characterizes Solomos's early Greek compositions, is lacking in the stereotyped and incantational dullness of this work.

Dionysios was proud of his ten-stanza "Ode for a First Mass," which had appealed to his teacher Pini. Its one hundred alternately rhymed lines, full of ecclesiastical and biblical imagery, are but a pious verse oration encouraging the new priest to chant the "mystic hymn," praise the greatness of the Lord, and offer the Sacraments to the faithful (II, 89–92). As its title indicates, this ode was inspired by the importance that Solomos ascribed to the Church and the first liturgy that a newly ordained priest celebrates. This poem is not just another exercise in versification. Its size and honesty of feeling betray a young and devout poet instinctively groping for the sublime. Under the spiritual tutelage of Alessandro Manzoni, the young Greek could not but grope toward the realm of faith.

A glance at the titles of numerous Italian sonnets that Solomos composed while in Zante, and even toward the end of his sojourn in Italy, would make a clergyman feel religious fervor and a layman wonder if the poet was a man of the cloth. With his own profoundly devout nature enhanced by the artistic achievement of Manzoni in the genre of devotional poetry, Solomos composed, or rather, improvised sonnet after sonnet about the details of the Christian faith, feasts of the Church, and even saints and clergymen.

Manzoni's *Sacred Hymns* (Inni Sacri) began appearing in print while Solomos was still in Italy (1815). Though Solomos's reaction to them was immediate and enthusiastic, it would be unfair to the budding poet to term it slavish. Inspired by the Italian poet's genuine feeling Solomos certainly was. But this influence was never manifested as unoriginal imitation.

The early *Sacred Hymns* contains the following poems: "The Nativity," "The Passion," "The Resurrection," "The Pentecost," "Maria's Name," and "Strophes for a First Communion." None of them is a sonnet. "The Nativity" consists of sixteen seven-line stanzas rhyming ababccd, or in similar combinations. The second is written in twelve rhyming octets, the third in sixteen septets again, and the fourth in eighteen octets. "Maria's Name" consists of twenty-one quatrains rhyming abab; and the First Communion poem consists of seven stanzas (six parts) of six, eight, nine, or twelve rhyming lines.[2]

Now if one turns to Solomos's religious poems in Italian one finds the same or similar titles: "The Birth of the Lord," "The Resurrection of the Lord," as well as "The Second Coming," "The Conception of the Virgin," "The Assumption of the Virgin," "Paradise," "Inferno," and so on (II, 126, 127, 133, 111, 129, 130, 133). All of these lyrics, however, are sonnets of Italian and Petrarchan variety, whereas Manzoni's were much lengthier odes and hymns. The conclusion that follows this comparison is that the young Greek was demonstrating a considerable amount of artistic freedom and initiative in composing his sacred sonnets. He did not imitate Manzoni's verse forms, nor did he limit the range of his subject matter to what the Italian Romantic had already done.

It could be observed here that Solomos's "telescoping," so to speak, into the sonnet form the material that the Italian poet had "stretched" into, say, eighteen octets (cf. the Resurrection poems of both), shows that the poet had a very sound sense of poetic economy fairly early. Indeed, rhetoric is not needed where genuine religious feeling can be invoked and communicated with economy of means and decorum.

As much as Manzoni and the various other Italian masters showed the way to Solomos, the Italian influence was not of the rigid and inflexible nature that normally results in artistic imitation. From his Italian models, Solomos received inspiration and encouragement and initiative to create his own style and vehicle of expression.

Solomos wrote some one hundred Italian sonnets. Four of these were composed in Italy, two actually being variations on the First Mass theme. Another thirty, on various subjects but mostly biblical and devotional, were improvised during 1818–22, at the parties of the youthful Zantiot group in Merkatis's house and other such occasions.[3] The notation that often appears, "with obligatory rhymes," is indicative of the pride and pleasure that Solomos and his friends derived from these nearly always spontaneous improvisations. These thirty sonnets made up the slim volume of *Poetic Improvisations* that L. Strani published without the poet's knowledge in 1822.[4]

Of the remaining sonnets, all but two of which were composed while Solomos was in Zante, nine are inspired by Solomon's "Song of Songs"—a kind of rough equivalent to Byron's "Hebrew Melodies"—several describe the Zantiot landscape, some are dedicated to friends, artists, or important personalities (Dante, Napoleon, Pope Pius VII, Saint Denis, and others), several are on devotional and biblical themes, as was mentioned earlier, and quite a few are parodies and burlesques of Dr. Roidis and his verse.

Of special interest are Solomos's sonnets "Against Bonaparte," and "Bonaparte," both rhyming very competently abba/ abba/ cdc/ ede (II, 142–43). Both were probably written before Napoleon's death on Saint Helena (1821), because the French ruler is harshly criticized for having caused so much death and destruction. The pious and refined Solomos would scarcely have done so if Napoleon were deceased.

"Bonaparte," which was probably improvised when Anthony Matesis wrote his on the same subject (there is considerable similarity in the rhyme schemes of both),[5] can be summarized as follows: Napoleon, who is responsible for so many catastrophes, bears a soiled name which had previously made people admire him. On the snowbanks of Moscow, where the blows of the enemy and his own passion bring him, there are bad omens for his overweening power. Nobody has sympathy for him, and may no new astrological gyration ever restore him to a better orbit, for every critical, logical mind will be mute.

The sonnet praising Dante is even more imaginative: whatsoever is stretched on the immense kingdom of the seas, whatsoever is born on the land, whatsoever feels and breathes, Dante had painted in his strange mind (II, 144). This sonnet shows how Solomos could express much in little space, for indeed his admiration for Dante is forcefully expressed, as well as the Italian's fantastic artistic grasp of this world, and of the three imaginary ones, in his *Divine Comedy*.

Similarly full of praise are the sonnets addressed to the Catholic Bishop L. Scacosz, who had expressed genuine enthusiasm when the Greek Revolution began; to Ugo Foscolo, to Petrarch, to the sculptor Canova, to Lord Guilford, and to several other friends. None of these lyrics, however, shows any signs of great artistry other than conventional competence, easy rhetoric, and skillful versification. Some of the endings were provided by friends; some were imitated, emulated, or even copied from sonnets of various Italian sonneteers, such as Vincenzo Monti, Angelo Mazza, Onofrio Minzoni, and others.[6] Often, the subject matter would be borrowed from an Italian original.

One of Solomos's few Italian improvisations in a form other than the sonnet is his "Ode to Venus." A combination of Italian "Arcadianism," Neoclassical pastoral, and nature idyll with pagan and Christian allusions, the improvised twelve-stanza ode is actually a happy song to joy, love, and procreation in nature. George Kalosgouros, the translator and editor of Solomos's Italian verse, found this poem "most beautiful" but untranslatable, for Greek was incapable of rendering the charm and richness of the original rhyme.

An idea of the idyllic description of nature and aura of jubilation that permeates this juvenile poem may be derived from a paraphrase of some of its sestets (rhyming ababcc). Sestet I: a divine breeze waves its wings over the sapphires of the still sea, trembling in a sweet, light intoxication, so that the One equal to nature may appear; the One [Venus] who will make the world fertile and beautiful. Stanza VII: Venus sees the wonders that appeared with her wonderful birth; pain should no longer feed men's souls with lamentation; and down here, witness of love, may the ethereal kingdom have a good time. Stanza IX: With this fertile smile that makes his wings vibrate, Eros comes down from Paradise, and the palpitation of hearts increases; for his appearance reflects an erotic fervor. Last Sestet (XII): Nectarine drops of joy you see drizzling down from the ether that sparkles with glitters; and you hear the hymns repeated in their sweet undulation by the waves breaking on the beaches (II, 148–51).

There is little profundity in the charming and pastoral rhetoric of the poem, but Solomos's description of nature is one of gusto and skill. The ode owes something to Classical or Neoclassical models on the same or similar subjects, as it probably does to painting.

On the other hand, the Classical allusions do not limit Solomos's initiative, nor do they subordinate his own Romantic and almost religious feeling at the miracle of procreation. The young Greek could not possibly have emulated in this simple ode the consummate poetic skill and Christian–Platonic thought that characterizes Edmund Spenser's "Epithalamion." If, however, a sense of proportion is maintained, one realizes that Solomos was already instinctively moving toward an idealistic, Neoplatonic, and moralistic handling of topics from ancient culture.

Rather than being merely artificial ornamentations and exterior to his verse, the elements of Classical Greek lore that Solomos most sparingly utilized in a few Italian poems, are carefully calculated motifs and even objective correlatives helping him to express his Weltanschauung and self.

II *The Greek Verse Translations*

Products of Dionysios's first and timid flirtation with the Greek Muse, his early translations are nevertheless important documents of his artistic development. Their versification, stanza form, and vocabulary betray a beginner practicing with determination and good care. Solomos's concern, at this stage, seems to be twofold. First, an exploration of the possibilities of the Greek language as he knew it; second, was the contemporary Greek idiom capable of expressing sophisticated, serious poetry?

A glance at the texts that Solomos turned into Greek, perhaps as early as 1818, shows that he was primarily concerned with descriptions of nature. A part of Metastasio's "The Spring" is turned into twelve quatrains, whose rhyming scheme is anything but regular or successful. The number of syllables in a line also varies widely (8—10), as does the language which is mostly colloquial with a few rather formal features. The same is true of the sixteen stanzas of Metastasio's "The Summer," an excerpt (I, 305—10).

Significant progress can be seen in the rendition of "A Fragment," again by Metastasio, into tercets (I, 310). Solomos's versification is remarkably improved; the rhyme pattern is correct, the sounds are more musical, and the number of syllables is steady, thus contributing to the quality of the rhythm; and even the subject matter is more elevated than the hitherto idyllic descriptions of nature. Lines like "Skill is missing and can't find me," and "Innocence is left to me only,/ I feel it within my breast deeply,/ But instead of bringing me any help,/ It crushes and cruelly smothers me," seem to be more than just an exercise in versification. Did Solomos pick this passage at random, or was he confessing or expressing on paper, echoing Metastasio's words, the difficulties and frustrations of an honest artist?

The eleven octets of Petrarch's "Ode," beginning with the refreshing image of "Water gurgling fresh and sweet," mark another successful step forward (I, 311—14). Solomos, impressed by the imagery of the poem, utilized it repeatedly in the future. Also the theme of death and the poet's serene confrontation of it, with faith and calm, are elements which Solomos used time and again in major and minor works.

In the same kind of octet (plus one sestet) Solomos rendered the Shakespearean "Song of Desdemona" (I, 314—16), beginning "The poor soul sat."[7] The Greek poet caught the spirit of the Elizabethan Bard and rendered it fairly accurately in an even and smooth Greek. The rhyme scheme, however, is still imperfect in this work, as it was in the rendition of Petrarch's ode. Instead of a normal rhyme pattern, all Solomos can achieve is abcbcded or even less polished combinations. Solomos's adherence to the original meaning and the limitations of his Greek created obstacles which would be overcome only in the future.

Poetic translation is perhaps one of the most intricate and demanding forms of literary composition. Solomos was not really trying to Hellenize these foreign poems. He was simply practicing, as an apprentice exercises hard and often in order to become a master.

Much later, when in Corfu, Solomos toyed with the idea of translating some Homer, as so many of his admired masters had done. Some twenty lines are extant from his version of rhapsody XVIII of the *Iliad* (I, 316—17). Even in their truncated and fragmentary form, Solomos's lines are considerably more faithful and poetic than similar attempts to turn Homer into modern Greek up to that time. With his example, Solomos stimulated poets of the immediate future to make Homer's masterpieces comprehensible to the people of modern Greece. Several of his disciples translated Homer and other classics with great success, a generation or two later, including Polylas.

Solomos also turned into a rhyming couplet (with fifteen—syllable lines) a triplet from Schiller, whose Greek title is "Amusia." Solomos's couplet can be rendered thus: "You possess the Muse if you take it into your warm bosom;/ To a barbarian's soul of stone it's but a heavy burden." Not only Schiller's spirit, but even diction and imagery, have been approximated in Solomos's Greek (I, 317).

Polylas, who wrote that he had heard many more lines from Solomos's *Iliad* than what he managed to record on paper,[8] observed that the poet had omitted six stanzas from Pietro Metastasio's "Spring" as well as fourteen from "Summer." In other words, Solomos omitted the erotic passages and concentrated on descriptions of nature, which were much more useful to a practicing apprentice.

A careful examination of these works, from a certain perspective, may enable a perspicacious reader to discern Solomos's ability— manifested so early—to isolate, so to speak, to apprehend, and then to translate into his own words the "essence" of a text, not its external form.[9]

III *The Early Greek Lyrics*

A first glimpse into Solomos's Greek lyrics of the Zantiot period (1818—28), after a prior examination of his Italian juvenilia and translations into Greek, is likely to make one wonder if all these works were composed by the same person.

Not a single sonnet was written in Greek by Solomos then, or at any other period of his life. Also there is no lyric devoted to or inspired solely by religion, or a saint, or any Christian holiday, though these elements were common in contemporary culture.

Few of the thirty lyrics, epigrams, and fragments of that period can be dated with certainty. The quality of their idiom, however, as well as of their over-all versification and technique, make us easily assume that their composition followed the early exercises, the translations into Greek. Two general observations can be made immediately about them. First, several of them deal with death, and even more express a feeling of calm melancholy as they are tinged with a fine touch of sadness. Second, the prevalent verse forms are genuinely and traditionally Greek, though some Italianate stanzas are introduced here and there, timidly and experimentally.

In the oral and written modern Greek literary tradition, which at that time Solomos was energetically absorbing, the young poet found inspiration, material, technique, and language. The verse stories, demotic songs, and pastoral idylls like "The Beautiful Shepherdess" of the Cretan Nicholas Drymitinos, various kinds of lyrics in meters and forms that had become naturalized Greek as early as the sixteenth century, were now his guides. To these one must add the lyrics of Christopoulos, Vilaras, Danelakis, Xanthopoulos, and all the Zantiots and other Greeks already mentioned.[10]

The most genuinely Greek of all the poetic vehicles of the period was the vernacular fifteen—syllable line, which is a distant descendant of the Classical dactylic hexameter. Fifteen—syllable verse rhyming in couplets had become extremely popular with the narrative *Erotokritos* and with several other successful poems from Crete and elsewhere. Solomos utilized it in his "Anthoula," "To a Maiden Brought up in a Convent," "Eurykome," "The Death of the Orphan Girl" (1822), and "The Death of the Shepherd" (1822). The last three were repeatedly published in anthologies and magazines in Greece and Europe during Solomos's lifetime, though often without his knowledge. The fact, however, attests to their popularity and to the poet's success with the demotic form and idiom.

A good idea of the form, language, and content of these lyrics may be formed from a reading of the following careful rendition of the four couplets entitled "Eurykome":

> "Ocean, when will I see the fair Eurykome?
> A long time has passed and she has not come to me.
> How often stooping on the rock, eager I and pale
> Mistook the foam of the sea for her white sail!
> Bring her back, bring her at last!"
>   That's what Thyrsis exclaims,
> And takes water from the sea, kisses it, and complains;

> Yet he doesn't know, miserable one,
> That he's kissing the wave,
> The same that has given her death as well
>   as a grave. (I, 59)

Another traditionally Greek stanza, the quatrain with alternating rhymes (abab) and seven or eight syllables per line, was generously used by Solomos at that period in all sorts of contexts and became the artistic vehicle that secured for the Zantiot poet a pre—eminent place in the Greek Pantheon and won for him fame everlasting and the honorable title, Poet of the Nation. For in that short, simple, unassuming quatrain, Solomos cast the material of his "Hymn to Liberty" and the "Lyrical Poem on the Death of Lord Byron."

This quatrain appeared for the first time in the lyrics "Desire," "Recollection," "To a Dying Friend," "The Dream," and the epigrams "The Cemetery," "You Don't Love Me," and "Calm," an imitation of Goethe. Variations in the number of syllables per line (8—10), as well as number and manner of stresses, are found in the quatrains of "Anger," "To Mr. George de Rossi," "To the Death of the Little Niece," and the poetic exercises or improvisations "Granddad's Shadow," "Swimming," and the like.

These variations of the four-line stanza, not found in earlier modern Greek verse, but common in Italian lyrics and songs, show how Solomos was working with both ethnic traditions at his disposal; drawing liberally from both, and putting, in the process, the stamp of his personal creation on whatever he produced.

Solomos was apparently attracted by the possibilities of the *ottava rima,* so he composed single stanzas for "The Flock," "The Two Tombs," "Hellas," and two for "Homer's Shadow." The language in them is good but not excellent, as is their versification, though technically correct. But the poet was merely experimenting with this stanza form.

Another experiment was the fragment "Ode to the Moon," one of the first modern Greek poems to be written in *terza rima.* Solomos attempted eighteen lines only and then gave up the project, because his Greek was in no condition then to provide the necessary rhymes, interior rhymes, and other intricate details of the successful Dantean *terza rima.* Suffice it to remember that even Shelley in his wonderful "Ode to the West Wind" and Byron in his "The Prophecy of Dante" had experienced difficulties with this form and were somehow forced to alter and adjust it to the realities of a language much less flexible than Italian. Solomos attempted this form, for a third time, in the Italian fragments of "The Death of a Young Poet," and produced some seventy-five imperfectly locked, actually disconnected lines. A fourth attempt was in an Italian satire. He then abandoned this form altogether.

Other, much more successful, poems were composed in quatrains with five-syllable lines and in sestets with six-syllable lines. Solomos performed miracles with fast-moving, airy, and melodious rhythms in his widely known "The Unknown Girl" and "The Little Soul." A mere recitation of these and other such poems turns to song—almost by itself. Before long they were set to exquisite tunes and were sung by all. Eventually "The Unknown Girl" inspired an aria in one of Greece's most popular operettas, which was but a paraphrase of Solomos's original nine quatrains.[11]

The meter and stanza form of this song had first been popularized by Thomas Danelakis, and then by John Vilaras, shortly before Solomos. Solomos, however, made it unforgettable because he associated it with the praise of a beautiful girl. This commonplace European tradition lost its conventionality and stylization in Solomos's songs. The female figure is not only exquisitely beautiful but ideally so. She is painted in light pastel colors, dressed in white, the very realization of a happy vision, almost a description of the Platonic idea of beautiful and pure womanhood. She is closely associated with nature; and simple, unsophisticated imagery of flowers, dew, grass, leaves, and the color of the sky are used in her depiction (I, 63—64). The lyric ends with the stanza with which it began: "Who is that girl/ That's coming down/ Dressed in white/ From the mountain?" No translation can give even the slightest impression of this lyric's beauty. Who is she, indeed? A friend, a wife, a lover, a daughter, an allegorical figure of something sublime? Solomos kept his audiences in purposeful suspense.

The image of another girl, Catherine Mavrogordatos, a six-year-old child of Chiot refugees who had stayed briefly in Zante and then left for England, inspired Solomos to compose his most charming song, "The Little Blonde Girl" (Xanthoula), the celebrated song which all Greeks learn and sing even before going to school. It is reported that days after its release, in manuscript form, of course, Zantiots came with mandolins and guitars and serenaded Solomos with a new song, his own "Xanthoula" (I, 65—66).

The first of its eight quatrains (abab) can be rendered thus:

> At eventide I saw her
> The little girl fair-tressed,
> As swiftly the boat took her
> Far to the distant West.

The poet then compares the ship to a flying dove sailing away, while friends wave at her from the shore and she keeps waving back. But soon the sight is lost in the horizon, and when kerchief and boat can be seen no longer, "The friends shed then a tear/ And the same happened to me," is all Solomos says in the way of expressing emotion. Two more stanzas explain that he is crying for the fair-haired Xanthoula and not for the small boat. With refugees coming from Greek islands and provinces that had experienced recent Turkish atrocities and who had lost everything they had under the sun, the poem had connotations far exceeding that of a child's going away. Even the theme of departure for the West to a people of emigrants, like these Greeks since Odysseus's time, was bound to touch again wounds that were hidden in many a lonely heart.

The theme of death was treated with exquisite tact in the four sestets of "The Little Soul." Edgar Allan Poe believed that the death of a beautiful and ideal woman was the best subject for great poetry; Solomos's Romanticism obsessed him with the idea of pretty little innocent children dying. During his life the poet maintained a most genuine affection and sympathy for children. In his own family, death had taken away, often in their infancy, most of his father's children by his first wife. His half-brother Robert had lost some, and his beloved Demetrios lost several. Solomos was profoundly moved by the deaths of these innocents, though he was never a father himself. Also, observant and sensitive as he was, Solomos had experienced the tragic affliction of mothers caused by the loss of their infants or children, and he often composed poems to relatives and friends inspired by such sad events. In "The Little Soul" (I, 62) the spirit of the child reaches the realm of the stars, but it does not know which one to enter. A little Angel, however, gives it an immortal kiss, and the child "shone like the dawn." With controlled emotion expressed in simple and soft words as children would have used, Solomos versified the idea that innocent children become stars when they die.

In the same spirit Solomos composed the four quatrains entitled "To the Death of the Little Niece." Vivid are his recollections of the infant—the three-year-old Elizabeth, daughter of Demetrios—suffering in her bed and finally expiring on January 6, 1825. "Sweet but deceitful were your parents' thoughts of you," the poet observes with chagrin, as he concludes with the mention of the dream that all parents have about their little girls: "They were thinking of a wreath for a wedding, but a different one is now worn by you" (I, 56).

The same tone of serene melancholy is set in all the verse requiems of Solomos. Addressing his close friend George de Rossi, who was in England when his father passed away (1828), the poet wrote a lyric which is a masterpiece in its own way, as an expression of the affection that father and son mutually cherished. The fourth and last quatrain describes the father's end as follows:

> But a moment before flying away
> Toward the realm of Heaven,
> Slowly did his hand wave
> As if for a final blessing. (I, 54)

The greatest and most powerful of Solomos's memorial lyrics of the Zantiot period is, undoubtedly, the one he wrote to defend the memory of Miss Maria Papageorgakopoulos, in 1826. A sensitive and cultivated young lady from the circle of Solomos's Zantiot acquaintances, she fell desperately in love with a musician from Venice.[12] The affair remained platonic, but Maria was driven to despair when she learned that the Venetian was already married, and she took poison. As is natural in a small and closed society, the news spread immediately, and the event was invariably interpreted by callous gossipers as Maria's act to cover the loss of her honor and the physical consequences. Solomos became furious when he heard the slander, for he knew the innocent girl well, and, no doubt, had often discussed topics of common interest with her. We know that she had learned all his poems and delighted in reciting or singing them.

Dionysios felt the need to compose a lyric defending the unfortunate suicide in which he would castigate, obliquely, the Zantiots for their promulgating false rumors which soiled the memory of a pure and innocent girl. Her idealism and courage also impressed him, as the idealism of his niece was to inspire him much later (1850). On the other hand, since the time of the composition of the "Hymn to Liberty," Dionysios had developed a deep sense of duty as a moralizer and teacher for his nation. The suicide of the innocent girl now offered him the opportunity to function not only as a lyricist but as a sage—a

Bard as well. Religious as he always was, Solomos hinted that the lady's only mistake was her violence toward her own life.

One may render three of its twelve quatrains competently, but freely, as follows:

> You used to sing all my songs,
> But this one you've left alone,
> Only this one you will never hear;
> As you are covered by the tomb-stone.
>
> Innocent girl! If honest tears
> Could with magic defeat death,
> I have shed for you so many,
> That you should now have breath.
>
> "Look deep into my soul, O Lord,
> That laments for its sin,
> And tell the slanderous world
> Whether other wounds lie therein."

The poem circulated widely, orally and in manuscript, and was generally acclaimed. Not only that, but the populace, realizing their own pettiness, starting visiting the cemetery to scatter flowers over her fresh grave—an indication of their complete reversal of feelings.

The critic Apostolakis, concluding his enthusiastic commentary of this poem, states that "The Poisoned Girl" is a "pure musical creation, like all of Solomos's songs. Though simple in its technique and meaning, it immediately captivates the person who hears it. No logical analysis can explore the secret of its power. It is found only in the enthusiasm and the ecstasy of the poet's soul before the living form; and the form appears pure in the song."[13]

A few general comments may be made about Solomos's nonpatriotic poems of the Zantiot period. With the exception of a few pieces which are poetic exercises, verses that came spontaneously, so to speak, to him were invariably inspired by deeply felt emotions. Light poems were composed on happy occasions, births of new babies, recoveries from illness, anniversaries, and the like. More profound ones were inspired by the loss of beloved persons. The best of all is inspired by a combination of sorrow, indignation, admiration, and other feelings; it is remarkable how Solomos controlled all of these feelings and expressed them in an appropriately suitable meter without losing, even for a moment, his sense of propriety, and without being carried away by the outpouring of his own powerful feelings. For the feelings are certainly there, and the audience is made to share them as if by magic.

"The Poisoned Girl," moreover, served a much broader social function than merely the communication of personal feelings and esthetic pleasure. In it Solomos assumed a didactic pose which, however, he felt profoundly. The people must learn, and the Bard must teach them. The combination of his quest for sensory delight and the search for the moral ideal that would make up the fabric of the verse at this period began to develop into something akin to an obsession. Solomos was by that time a "poet, a revolutionary, and a teacher," as Dr. Basil Vlavianos put it.[14] The facile themes and melodies of his early years as a poet would soon be given up, and the maturing artist would commit himself to the service of this nation's spiritual needs. And there were many such needs in Greece of the 1820's.

CHAPTER 7

The National Bard

I "The Hymn to Liberty"

E VEN WHEN only a student, Solomos believed that sentiment alone was not enough for the conception and eventual realization of a major work. Young Solomos's characteristic remark to the venerable Monti was that the poet should be a logical and profound thinker, in addition to being a sensitive and eloquent artisan of verse.

One can imagine with what interest, burning anxiety, and strong sentiments the young Greek poet followed the dramatic events of the Revolution of 1821. Would it prove to be, like so many others before it, just a spontaneous but short-lived uprising against the all-powerful oppressor, which would be stamped out and forgotten as rapidly and easily as it had started? Or would it develop into an all-out and decisive war to secure freedom, human dignity, and a national identity, a now-or-never liberation movement? Events soon proved that the latter was the case this time.

While Solomos eagerly awaited the news from the motherland, the hitherto wretched and uncouth Greek peasant-warriors, mountaineers, and formerly peaceful merchants with their small ships, were now proving themselves worthy descendents of the historical figures of the Greek past.

The poorly equipped, undersized, and irregular bands of shepherds, farmers, and sailors had begun to shake the edifice of a mighty empire and to defeat its great armies and fleets again and again, with unprecedented determination and courage. Yes, it was a now-or-never war; it was a holy cause.

What was the duty of a twenty-five-year-old Greek under the circumstances? To join the fight, of course. And that is what Solomos did. As a poet, he chose to fight with his pen, not with pistols and swords which he had never touched before. The purely military contributions Solomos could make to the cause of Greek independence would be ridiculously insignificant. The immediate consequences to his beloved ones and himself were easily predictable. But as a writer he could wield the most powerful of all weapons, his talent, and achieve much more in the long run.[1]

If Solomos were to propagate the sacred ideas of this war to friendly fellow Christians in the West, if he were to inspire more enthusiasm and faith and preach unity and unselfish cooperation to the unruly but stubborn warriors, he would then do something no one else had done. Reghas Pheraios and the other prophetic versifiers of Greek freedom were long dead. But Liberty needed a Bard to proclaim her to Greece and to the whole world. This Bard would be the hitherto composer of Italian sonnets, Greek idylls and requiems, and "Society verse," Dionysios Solomos, the peace-loving intellectual and esthete son of "Old Tobacco."

Solomos composed over one hundred and sixty quatrains of trochaic tetrameters alternating with seven-syllable lines. Some sources have it that he was writing under the influence of Italian Romanticism, in general, and Manzoni and his or others' techniques in particular.[2] It is true that many of the ideals of Italian and Western Romanticism are in the background (the quest for national identity, independence, popular culture, and the like), but most of Solomos's immediate and available models were genuinely Greek. One does not have to turn to Manzoni, whose "Triumph of Liberty" (c. 1801) was suppressed and never published before Solomos's death, to find a source.[3] Nor did Dionysios imitate the *terza rima* of the Italian poem, or its divisions into cantos, or its generally discursive recitation. On the other hand, details in imagery, especially related to the allegorical depiction of Liberty, temptingly echo Manzoni's, as does Solomos's style of notes appended to the poem. But that was a more or less general practice at that time, for Byron, Shelley, and others, added notes to, or prefaced, their long works with "arguments."

There is no doubt that Solomos was inspired by Greek literary sources to write this long lyric, in addition, of course, to the dramatic developments of the war itself and to his psychological identification with the Greeks.

The opening of the "Hymn to Liberty" utilizes the imagery borrowed from Anthony Martelaos's patriotic hymn to France, to Napoleon, and the like, whom the Zantiot radical had considered a would-be liberator of Greece. Solomos also echoes Reghas Pheraios's "War-Song" and other revolutionary lyrics, as well as Thomas Danelakis, who had imitated both Martelaos and Reghas in exactly the same verse form.[4] The original model and source of all these, and other Greek political versifiers, was the French "Marseillaise" by Leconte de Lisle. This revolutionary anthem had been very popular in Zante and elsewhere since shortly before the turn of the century, and many of its numerous Greek imitations were sung to its tune. The pristine source of inspiration for all these literary effusions was, of course, man's love for freedom and self-dignity, which had been dramatically reiterated by the Enlightenment.

The poem begins with a magnificent and dramatic address to Liberty:

-1-

> I know you by the trenchant gleaming
> That radiates from your sword,
> I know you by the sight whose beaming
> Measures the earth as victor lord.

-2-

> Sprung from Grecian bones scattered
> Hallowed on every historic vale,
> With your pristine valor unshattered,
> Liberty, hail to you, hail! (I, 71)

Solomos divided his bulky poem into several parts by repeating the second stanza three times and the first stanza once more, at various intervals. This kind of refrain provides a transition from one group of quatrains to another without undue stressing of the poem's logical order.

As Polylas, Jenkins, Tomadakis, and others have explained, the early stanzas refer to the past up to 1821, when Liberty was buried alive, as it were, in the tomb of the legendary heroes, waiting for help and an invitation to return.[5] But fear and tyranny reigned supreme, and Liberty in desperation started begging for help from strangers, only to be laughed at, or cheated with empty promises. This situation has now changed, Solomos emphatically asserts, as he answers Reghas's famous call to arms and Byron's sad remarks about Greek servility:

-15-

> Yes, but your sons, your offspring
> Are now fighting with all their breath,
> And unceasingly are seeking
> Either Victory or Death. (I, 73)

Strophes 17—34 describe the reaction of the world to the awakening
of Liberty and her stormy return to Greece. Heaven and earth and most
lands hail the event with profound joy. Even the Heptanesians, who
enjoy "false freedom," join in the general jubilation. The Lion of Spain
gets up as if to roar approvingly, and the United States feels joy:

-22-

Most heartily was gladdened
George Washington's brave land;
For the iron bonds remembered,
Her old slavery's cruel brand. (I, 74)

England's Lion, however, roars angrily toward the direction of
Russia; and the Austrian eagle, which has been torturing the Italians,
screams fearfully with rage. Oblivious to all threats and difficulties,
Liberty proceeds with determination:

-38-

On and on her maddened sally
Through the woods a pathway traced;
Up the mountain, through the valley,
Spreading terror, death, and waste. (I, 76)[6]

After these general comments and the creation of the appropriate
atmosphere of violence, warfare, courage, and sacrifice, quatrains
35—74 focus on details of the siege and storming of Tripolitza, the
Turkish provincial capital of the Peloponnese; and the battles and
events (even the Greek abuses) that followed it. Solomos describes the
slaughter and general havoc with a great flair for realism and pictorial
representation:

-50-

Such a large host had gathered
Springing up from the earth,
Those that were unjustly slaughtered
By the Turkish wrath and strength. (I, 79)

Then the images of horror recede, and a fresh breeze blowing on the
Greek flag with the cross signals a victory:

-73-

Breeze of morning, cool and balmy
On Crescents you breathe no more,
Quit the pagan star and calmly
On the CROSS your spirit pour. (I, 83)

Quatrains 75–87 briefly mention the recent (1823) siege of Corinth, and the transformation of the pastoral plain into a battlefield. And then follows Solomos's famous "reply to Byron's lament that fair Greek girls should be mothers of slaves: the poet pictures the girls who are dancing in the shade, and rejoices to think that their breasts shall afford the milk of courage and freedom."

Solomos's pride at the courage of his fellow Greeks makes him add one of his few direct allusions to ancient Greek history in order to compare his compatriots to Leonidas's Spartans:

-78-

Rise, three hundred, rise returning
To the lands which once you knew,
Look at your children learning
To act exactly as you would do. (I, 84)

Stanzas 88–122 abound in biblical and Christian allusions and clusters of imagery as Liberty moves on to Missolonghi, and, embraced by Religion, repulses the Turkish besiegers and destroys them at the Battle of the Acheloos during Christmas (1822). As the Moslem host of cavalry and infantry are lost in the turbulent river, the poet wishes he had Moses's voice to praise and thank the Lord for his assistance.

In the same spirit the hymn proceeds to extol the astonishing exploits of Captain Kanaris on sea (quatrains 123–128), and bids the shadow of the Patriarch Gregory V–whom the Turks had murdered in his cathedral in April, 1821–to rejoice now that so many important infidels had drowned. God will punish them for their outrages, the mutilation of the holy man's body. Liberty, however, now bids the poet to keep his peace and, with worrying glances toward Europe, begins to address the Greek warriors.

Liberty harangues (actually echoing Solomos's own honest admonitions found in letters) the individualistic, undisciplined and disunited Greeks to stop their internecine feuds that only help the enemy and make the Europeans think that the Greeks do not deserve freedom (stanzas 141–149). The ever present goddess of disunion (Eris) is forcefully described by the idealistic poet in Stanza 144:

Discord, with her wily offers
Of a scepter which strongly lures
Each man, as she smilingly proffers
Telling him, "Take it; it is yours." (I, 95)

Finally Solomos, through Liberty's voice, appeals to the royal heads of the Christian countries in Europe to help their fellow Christians in Greece. He does that indirectly by challenging them to oppose the Christians openly, and side, if they dare, with the Moslem Turks:

-155-

Images of the Most High,
Can't you feel her [Greece's] agonies?
Never silent was her cry
For so many centuries.

-157-

What then? Can you leave alone
Those who fight for Liberty;
Or will you destroy it, if won,
To expedite your Policy?

-158-

If this is your firm decision,
Here, before you stands the Cross!
Crush it, Monarchs, to oblivion,
Crush it, help to wreak our loss. (I, 97)

The conclusion of the poem was declared unfitting by one critic, on esthetic grounds.[7] But one only knows too well what disunity and foreign cynicism have caused to the Greeks in their long history. The poem would have been the product of an effete esthete if it did not contain these powerful appeals for unity and faith in a common cause. For no major poem on freedom can be based merely on abstractions, praise, and wishful thinking. Solomos, as an intellectual product of the Enlightenment, was trained in logical argumentation and realistic attitudes. As he was living outside Greece proper, he could observe all happenings from a certain perspective that afforded him the opportunity to be objective. The "Hymn" could not be a sustained and grandiose exercise in ambitious poetics alone. It would have to be a document, a gospel, a manifesto, a loud and irrevocable declaration to friend and foe. And this it was.

The success of the "Hymn" was immediate. Copies were sent overseas. Trikoupis, aflame with enthusiasm, was dispatched to Missolonghi bringing a copy to Lord Byron, the self-styled commander of the crack Suliot detachment. But it was too late. The Englishman had died a few days earlier.[8]

But the gods of Greece were on the side of Solomos and his countrymen. By 1825 the "Hymn to Liberty" had been published in Greek, French, English, and Italian. Many Greeks and non-Greeks read or heard it, or practiced their Greek on it, in Europe and even in America; and the reaction was always one of deep satisfaction, pride, and enthusiasm.[9]

Chateaubriand and Lamartine applauded it with delight. Manzoni hailed it with pride and spread Solomos's fame in Italy.[10] Victor Hugo remarked with touching sympathy: "The young poetry singing the young freedom."[11] It is even reported, but not verified, that the great Goethe read his copy and proclaimed Solomos the "Byron of the East."[12]

The Greek and European press announced its publication, or reviewed it most favorably, often thanks to the energies of men like Fauriel and Trikoupis. Even in America the Hellenist Cornelius Felton praised the "Hymn" as a masterpiece and compared Solomos to the ancient martial and patriotic poets Simonides and Alkaios. Equally favorable were the comments of New York University Professor Corby, who proclaimed Solomos the Pindar of modern Greece.[13]

Philhellenic sentiment was particularly genuine and strong in the young and liberal republic of the United States, whose intellectuals composed over one hundred hymns, odes, and all sorts of lyrics in support of the Greek Revolution, in the years 1821–30. The major poets of the pre-Poe period—Bryant, Brooks, Halleck, Percival, Wetmore, and Woodworth—had all composed philhellenic, Byronic pieces. At least two of the numerous anonymous poets who did so after 1825 must have seen Solomos's "Hymn" in the original or in a translation, because the subject matter, imagery, and arguments of their long poems remind one of the Greek poem; and their stanza form and meter are identical with the "Hymn to Liberty."[14]

One of the American commentators on the most famous of these philhellenic effusions, "Marco Bozzaris," a long ode by Fitz-Greene Halleck, characteristically observed that Halleck's poem, as a celebrated propaganda weapon, "must have been worth at least a frigate to the Greeks."[15] There is no exaggeration in this statement. By analogy one may understand how many frigates or regiments Solomos's own poem was worth to the Greeks. The civilized world had evidence to support the claims of Greece as a nation reborn out of its own ashes.

It is not possible to estimate the contribution of this hymn to the Greek cause. Suffice it to mention here that Sir George Canning had read Solomos's poem and quoted the lines, "Sprung from Grecian bones scattered . . . ," in a speech. The same source has it that the British prime minister had read the "Hymn" the day he signed the protocol of London, which guaranteed Greek independence.[16]

From the purely artistic side, its success was not less. The "Hymn" was the greatest and most ambitious poem written in modern Greek for centuries. Its vocabulary and metrics were not always perfect, but they were considerably better than anything else in that genre. The signs of hasty composition were certainly there. But since this one time Solomos had allowed his emotions to be recollected, not in tranquillity, but when he was overwhelmed by his passion for freedom, the result was spontaneous, vigorous, spirited, and easily flowing numerous lines.[17]

In a poem of so many stanzas not all of them can be of equal quality, not all expressions equally felicitous. Some connecting passages, rhetorical outbursts, a few images in poor taste, some unfortunate linguistic liberties, the organization of the material, and even some echoes or borrowings from other poets, Greek and foreign, have been cited by erudite philologists either as minor weaknesses or as serious flaws.

The truth is that Solomos had produced a series of pictorial stanzas whose audiovisual imagery was of the highest caliber, even though in 1823 he was still in his period of apprenticeship. After the completion of the "Hymn"—a major work in most respects—Solomos had to move on to achievements of a higher level. The echoing directly or indirectly of Manzoni, Monti, Ariosto, Parini, Foscolo, Dante, Milton, Byron, Homer, Virgil, and other "moderns and ancients" should not be taken as a weakness at all. On the contrary, Solomos in so doing experimented with the verbal expressions and images of these masters to see how they sounded in Greek. It is not artistic paucity that made, on the other hand, Solomos echo the stilted but patriotic lines of Reghas and Martelaos. By doing so the young poet joined the invisible chain of cultural tradition, so to speak, and inherited the lighted torch. No poet can exist and function outside the literary tradition of his culture, as T. S. Eliot implies in "Tradition and the Individual Talent." And in this way Solomos joined the Hellenic tradition and continued it. The result was both impressive and encouraging: modern Greek, Solomos's own language, was capable of emulating the language of the great masters. But there was need for improvement, both quantitative and qualitative.

Jenkins has correctly summarized the role of the borrowed element in the "Hymn":

The overweight of borrowing from abroad, while it might spoil the poem as an individual masterpiece, was exactly what was required for the "cultivation" (the expression is Solomos') of the tongue; *and the ingenuity and taste required to translate into Greek the nobler political ideas expressed in the cultivated languages of Europe* were the most salutary faculties that could have been brought into play [italics mine].[18]

Perhaps the one negative legacy that this poem left to Solomos himself, who now virtually woke up to find himself famous, was the idea that poetic greatness had to, and could, be achieved only in conjunction with the expression of patriotic and religious fervor. For if that was the case, Solomos was unconsciously imposing undue limitations on his artistic range and particular talent.

II *The "Lyrical Poem on the Death of Lord Byron"*

Solomos was with friends when Trikoupis's letter with the sad news was brought to him: "Byron is dead!" As Tennyson, Carlyle, Lamartine, and Hugo later recorded their shock at the realization that Byron was no more, so did Dionysios turn pale, experiencing a profound feeling of personal loss.[19]

Once again the emotions which welled from his heart were released in a tribute to the great man and his beloved Greece. It is said that Solomos extemporized a quatrain and left his company in grief:

-1-

Liberty, cease for a moment
Striking with your sword,
But approach here to lament
By the body of the noble lord. (I, 101)

Solomos committed more than two hundred stanzas to paper before feeling the need to surcease. Having hardly finished the polishing and copying of his "Hymn," the young poet was forced by circumstances immediately to embark on an equally demanding task. Solomos did not have time to think of a new verse form and a new approach to his themes. Nor was he allowed a respite during which he could continue practicing and improving his Greek. The poem had to be written quickly and with whatever means the hard-pressed poet could marshal.

Thus most of the weaknesses, as well as merits, of the "Hymn" reappear in the "Lyrical Poem," which may be considered a companion piece to the previous composition, and a repeat performance.

Solomos was aware of the imperfections resulting from his hasty composition, overflow of sentiment, and bulk and disparity of material. True to his quest for the ideal, he kept revising it for years, reworking several stanzas, or composing new ones to substitute for others. There are two manuscripts extant, as well as numerous variations, and an enormous number of critical comments and corrections in Italian and in Greek. This fact attests to the critical insights that the poet was rapidly developing. The poem, however, was never committed to print during Solomos's lifetime, though it circulated widely in manuscript copies and later on was set to a solemn elegiac melody.

Tomadakis believes that the change in British foreign policy, which after 1825 was to support the Greek cause, made the "Lyrical Poem on the Death of Lord Byron" seem unfairly critical of England and biased.[20] In addition, one must mention the respect Solomos had for Lord Guilford, who had tactfully suggested that stanzas betraying undue anti-British bias should be removed even from the "Hymn."[21] Trikoupis also was a mutual friend of both aristocrats and his wishes may have dissuaded Solomos.

The final text of the poem consists of one hundred and sixty-six quatrains, identical in metrics and other features to those of the "Hymn." An idea of the rich, imaginative and powerful contents may be derived from the following analysis of its organization.

Stanzas 1—5 make up the general introduction. In it Liberty is bid to stop the war and lament Byron. The latter's name is associated with the Suliots, whom he nominally commanded, and with their previous leader, Markos Botsaris, who had fallen heroically in 1823. Quatrains 6—18 are a kind of appraisal of Byron as a poet, as an idealist and lover of freedom. In this connection, Solomos has the opportunity to refer to America and to present her, once again, as the country of the free:

-16-
"Every land," he complains,
"Is enslaved"—but there is one,
Where in honor man remains,
Away from here, afar. (I, 103)

Stanzas 19—32 praise Greek freedom, Byron, and those who fight for it, while Solomos curses the tyrants who oppose it. The fame of the Englishman has moved ahead of him, and the various Greek groups wonder which one the new ally is going to join. Missolonghi is Byron's wise and symbolic choice (stanzas 31—51).

The supernatural element is imaginatively used in Byron's welcoming by the war dead, headed by the Patriarch. Byron then meditates as he watches Greece rejoice at his arrival and feels sorry for what their disunity has cost the warriors. Solomos, acting as political prophet, warns them to avoid the trouble of Erinys, for they will either wind up under a foreign monarch or will be destroyed by the enemy (stanzas 52—82).

Solomos's obsession with Greek factionalism was entirely justified, for both bitter predictions were to come true in a few years. A Bavarian king ruled the liberated Greeks with an iron hand, while the majority of the Greek people remained in territories and provinces still under Turkish control.

Quatrains 83—106 constitute a long digression in which the poet explores the historical degradation of his nation as a result of eternal discord, from Polybius's time until that of Byron, who had himself complained about the deplorable status of contemporary Greeks. Solomos considers England a powerful and haughty oppressor, which did not sympathize with the aspirations of Greece, as Byron did. Then the wars of the Suliots against Ali Pasha and the self-sacrifice of the women at Zalongo are mentioned, and the warriors of 1821 are praised as worthy of their ancestors, despite their selfishness and pride.

Stanzas 107—33 present Byron spending the night by the tombs of Botsaris and another hero, Kyriakoulis Mavromichalis, and thinking about the future. Byron's pilgrimage to the consecrated ground inspires him with a fervent desire to join the war. He thinks of Sophocles and Aeschylos as warriors for freedom and of children becoming brave fighters under the inspiration of battle hymns. Byron remembers his daughter in England, asking him to return to her mother, as a hero respected by all. But while the ship sails home, the poet cannot hear the murmur of the waves, for he is dead.

Quatrains 134—60 contain Greece's lament for Byron, whom Solomos pictures as having visions of his child and of Liberty. Napoleon is mentioned, in this passage, as the "Man of the Century," who had also died before realizing a one-time idea of becoming the liberator of Greece. Solomos contrasts to the attitudes of these great men the pettiness of some contemporary Frenchmen who had rejoiced when Greece suffered a major catastrophe at Psara. But they are alive, whereas Byron is now in Hades.

Stanzas 161—66 portray the shadows of the war dead welcoming Byron among them and asking him anxiously about the fate of their beloved Greece. The poet, solemnly observing their wounds and suppliant faces, declares, once again:

-166-

Greece once more Discord is plaguing;
If you can the two of them sever,
BY THE WORLD THE ALL-CONTAINING
Your name shall live forever. (I, 132)

Criticisms similar to those leveled at the "Hymn" were repeated about this poem, too.[22] The language is not very careful, the organization is faulty, the allusions too numerous; the echoes of works by Byron, Milton, and Gray are alien to a Greek poem; the references to Byron's daughter have no place in such a poem; and so on.

But Solomos was actually writing a verse eulogy, and in it he thought he should show familiarity with the life and achievements of the deceased person. That he chose to mention little Augusta, waiting for her father back home, is not surprising at all to those who know Solomos well. As has already been mentioned, his love for children and his feelings for their sorrow were repeatedly manifested in his poems, letters, and actions. After all, it is very touching, almost pathetic, for the reader to momentarily think of Byron as a father who will be missed by his little daughter.

Also, Solomos's references to Botsaris and other warriors are in harmony with the idea of presenting Byron as a hero of the war—a hero who, like Solomos himself, had fought for Greek independence wielding the same weapon, his pen. Stanza 100, referring to the brave Suliot women who fell over the precipice of Zalongo to avoid capture and humiliation, utilized imagery from Thomas Gray's "The Bard," in which the bearded and venerable poet contemplates the river Conway into which he is going to jump for reasons similar to those of the Suliot women. The heroic women

-100-

Were generously inspired
By the same honorable feeling
That the Brave Bard had experienced
When at Conway he was staring. (I, 119)

The echoes or references to Milton (stanzas 14—15, 42—44) and to Byron's poems (stanzas 16, 19), the notes and elsewhere, are anything but irrelevant, as Tomadakis wrongly complains.[23] How could Solomos write about a foremost English poet without showing a knowledge and appreciation of his poetry and that of other English artists? Moreover, what Jenkins had observed in relation to Dantean and Classical echoes in the "Hymn" is certainly true of this work as well: Solomos was trying to show that Greek could emulate the poetic idiom of these masters. In all fairness to the young Greek, we must agree that he was successful in this respect. As a Westernized Greek, Solomos would, of course, utilize elements that were not part of the limited cultural awareness of many Greeks.

Before we leave this magnificent poem—actually one of the earliest and greatest verse tributes to Byron so soon after his death—we may form an idea of how Solomos imagined Byron paying tribute to Botsaris, in Jenkins's free but melodious imitation of Solomos in Victorian diction:

-113-

Here no foot-fall strikes the ear;
Only athwart the funeral stone
Falls that mighty shadow's finger,
Slender, silent, and alone;

-114-

So the cypress, tree of death
Lays his long, black shadow down,
When no gentle zephyr's breath
Wakes to stir his young, green crown.

-115-

Say, thou valiant, wither tending
Are those noble thoughts of thine,
As they turn in never-ending
Stream, by Marco's lowly shrine? (I, 121)[24]

Stanzas like these give the "Lyrical Poem" an appropriately solemn and elegiac tone, for it is not an epic, or a historical poem, as some philologists would have it. It is the subjective, personal, and lyrical expression of a young and gifted idealist in memory of a celebrated and greater compeer.

III   Shorter Lyrics

The death of Markos Botsaris on the battlefield, during his successful storming of the Turkish camp at Karpenisi, near the historic Plataea

(1823), made Solomos attempt a heroic ode soon after the event. It must be observed here that the poet had avoided praising individual warriors, despite their exploits, in single poems. It is doubtful that he would have done so for Botsaris, had the young and humble Suliot not sacrificed his life for his ideals.

Solomos, who was virtually up to his neck with the conception, composition, and revision of the almost four hundred quatrains that he had composed for his two major patriotic poems in less than two years, found the energy and time to write nine rhyming quintets (abbcc) in honor of the brave Greek.

The imagery of the ode recreates the allegorical figures Fame, Envy, and Glory—Solomos's debt to Dante and other traditional sources—which disappear when Botsaris dies and, significantly, only Glory remains by his tombstone. Homer's *Iliad*, XXIV, supplies then the idea of Priam rescuing the body of his son Hektor for a proper burial. Similarly, the modern Greeks bury and mourn their defender in great and universal clamor. Then there is a gap, as the perfectionist Solomos did not have the opportunity to create an appropriate transitional passage to connect the contemporary funeral scene with the imaginable future, which, in other words, would have suggested eternity, and the hero's lasting, eternal fame. The last quintet hints that a clamor comparable to that of the funeral will be heard on Doomsday (I, 137–38).

The poem was subtitled a "fragment," but it is actually almost complete. A lyrical idea such as the immortality of a hero's name could not possibly offer material for a longer work, unless the poet were to resort to rhetoric or historiography in verse, neither of which did appeal to Solomos.

The technique of description and idealization shows slight progress over the two other poems. The Italianate stanza form, with its nine-syllable line, indicates that Solomos knew better than to utilize the much shorter and rapid line of the "Hymn" in this elegy. A decent poem in most respects, Solomos's ode "To Markos Botsaris" can hold its own, even in translation, if compared to Halleck's lengthy "Marco Bozzaris" and to James Gordon Brooks's and John H. B. Latrobe's lyrics extolling the character and exploits of the Suliot chieftain.[2 5]

Tomadakis commented intelligently on this poem by stating that

Here we find ourselves far from the didactic verse and the inducement, by means of admonition, to appeasement (or concord). The poet offers the great moral in another manner: This is the mission of the great man,

to fall fighting for the People. The Christian justification is not related
any longer to the pious, the saintly living, the just, the righteous, but to
the one who sacrifices, though he loves it, his own soul. He is the
justified one.[26]

Solomos did, indeed, share this new spiritual and intellectual
attitude toward the subject of his art. The tragic events of the war made
him mature early with respect to patriotism and the true essence of
nationalism. The ultimate sacrifice for freedom was not something that
could be turned into verse on the basis of a singled-out individual case.
Such a sacrifice, a catholic, a universal phenomenon, where the spirit of
the whole nation finds its best manifestation, was something that
transcended the boundaries and limitations of personal heroics.

The savage destruction of Psara, a diminutive island that had
wholeheartedly dedicated its ships and the souls of its sailors to the idea
of freedom, now or never, inspired Solomos to express the universality
of the theme of sacrifice in his most telling and famous epigram. "To
Psara" (1824–25), though composed in an Italianate ten-syllable line,
expressed the quintessence of valor and sacrifice with Solomos's
proverbial calm and lyrical intensity:

> On Psara's desolate, blackened stone
> Glory silently walks all alone
> Meditating her sons' noble deeds,
> And wears a wreath on her hair
> Made of such few and scattered weeds
> That were left over there. (I, 139)

"Neither pathos nor imagination are its characteristics," observes
Apostolakis; "Only idealism is."[27] "It is, as we should expect, very
short—only six lines, but in them harmony of structure, perfect
expression of idea, natural and touching imagery, a capacity for making
each word tell, and yet all combining in extreme simplicity, make the
epigram a masterpiece," comments Jenkins.[28]

The "Hymn to Liberty," for all its powerful and spirited descriptions, begins to sound dated by comparison to this epigram. With it
Solomos shows his ability, for the first time, to capture the poetic
moment and turn it into poetry of essence. Glory is no longer simply an
allegorical device. She is the spirit and form of the poem.[29] Names,
numbers, details have no place now, as expressions of horror, despair,
and determination are suggested, not directly communicated, in a
manner that would have won the approval of Simonides.

CHAPTER 8

Satires and Prose

I *Light Verse*

SERIOUS SATIRES are, by nature, didactic. Light and comic ones, on the other hand, normally are well-meant attempts to provide entertainment for a group, at the expense of one or more of its most vulnerable members.

Solomos composed not less than one dozen Greek and Italian verse satires, and parodies, on Dr. Roidis, as was mentioned earlier. What must impress the reader at this point is the fact that these numerous, and often lengthy compositions, were accomplished in the same period and, in some cases, almost simultaneously with Solomos's major lyrics and patriotic poems.

The portrait of the poet acquires another dimension, his personality is further explored, and our understanding of Solomos the man and the poet is substantially aided by these occasional pieces, which are akin in nature to much of the "Society verse" of the Age of Reason.

Solomos emerges from these lines as a witty, fun-loving, observant, and sharp-tongued Zantiot. As Solomos is following the well-established and rich satiric tradition of the Zantiot Greeks (Koutouzis, Gouzelis, and others), he is not likely to impress us as an innovator. His contributions to this genre, however, poured new blood, so to speak, into this sceptic custom, enriched it, and encouraged others to continue it.

Verse form is the heroic couplet in eight-syllable lines, rhymes are facile, and vocabulary is the Zantiot patois, with numerous local idioms, mannerisms, and Italian words and expressions. "New Year's Day" (260 lines); "The Medical Council" (267 lines); and "The Visit," also known as "The Gallows" (in two versions of 110 lines each) were all written around 1824, when, ironically, Solomos was busily working on his lengthy hymns.

In all these works Solomos uses stereotype criticisms of medical doctors: greed, avarice, cajolery to patients, quackery, and the like. Dr.

Roidis is the epitome of all of these and, in addition, his services to Apollo, the god of poetry, are as ludicrous as those to Hippokrates. His pompous style was parodied in Italian sonnets such as "The Apotheosis"; "Imitation of the Style of Dionysios Roidis"; and, among others, "To the Most Honorable Dr. Dionysios Count Roidis, Professor of I Don't Know What," which begins a poem of one hundred light lines in *terza rima.* Roidis's poetic genius was also ridiculed in the sixteen quatrains of another comic work in Italian.

The most interesting of these early satires is probably "The Medical Council." Roidis's own nephew is gravely ill, and the doctor-poetaster runs to see him in his sister's house. There is very comic expostulation with several characters, and other doctors who come to offer their services. Dr. Tayiapieras and many other Greek and foreign practitioners all offer their opinions in Greek, Italian, Latin, or even French (Tayiapieras had studied in France) and contribute to a general confusion—the main comic idea. Roidis antagonizes everybody, and at the end, when the child is almost dead, the other doctors leave perplexed while Roidis exclaims in triumph that he has outwitted them all.

Much must have been true in this innocuous story, as much was true in "The Dream," a considerably more caustic and passionate poem. In 1826 a despicable and corrupt man who had amassed a fortune, John Martinengo, died. His pompous and showy funeral upset the righteous and austere Solomos who, full of indignation, composed a satire to castigate the avarice and cruelty of the man. In a dream the poet has the satirist Koutouzis come from the dead to enumerate the vices of Martinengo.

Jenkins has rendered thus some of its biting couplets:[1]

> Mercy banished out of door
> With the widow and the poor,
> Cruelty came in her place,
> Hardening thy youthful face.
> She it was that counselled thee
> To steal the bread of poverty,
> And the interest to set
> At four times the initial debt. (I, 295)

Finally, when the priest himself attempts to attack the coffin, the poet exclaims in agony, "Don't! He's dead!" and wakes up drenched in his sweat. This satire appealed to the Heptanesians, for they knew Martinengo and believed that Solomos had not exaggerated the situation. The poem circulated widely, and its popularity attests to Solomos's ability to function as a social satirist as well, in addition to his innocuous practice of the genre with Roidis and other friends.

II *"The Woman of Zakynthos"*

A similar central theme dominates another satirical composition that Solomos was working on at the same time and later (1826–29), a social, impersonal, and allegorical satire which he left in the form of Greek prose. No title was given to it, but Polylas, who published a passage from it in the *Found Remains* (1859), gave it the name "The Woman of Zakynthos."

This prose work was published in its entirety only as late as 1927, and ever since editors have used the term "chapter" for each of its ten parts. The distribution of words, as well as the style and diction, found in each numbered paragraph of a chapter (ranging from 37 to 7), indicate that the material was meant to be turned to stanzas of verse. Sometimes there is enough material for a "large" stanza, perhaps an *ottava.* More often, however, the contents of one such paragraph would only suffice for considerably shorter units, probably quatrains, or fifteen-syllable lines rhyming in couplets. The manuscript contains a sestet of six-syllable lines in Chapter 5 (which later became part of draft I of "The Free Besieged"), and some of its lines almost form recognizable verse forms. The whole narrative, however, is completely devoid of witticisms, of any comic instances whatsoever, or of humor. This did not prevent the often misleading Jenkins from declaring that the long satirical poem Solomos intended to do "would have been something in the style of *Don Juan.* "[2] Would Byron's *magnum opus* be known at all today if it were not for its numerous cases of bathos, witticism, sarcasm, comedy, and general humor? Little if any comedy can be found in Solomos's prose, whose over-all tone is much like Saint John's in his *Apocalypse.*

The story is narrated by a monk, Dionysios, and there is no doubt that the author identified with this persona. The plot consists of a kind of general introduction, followed by an allegorical episode with the Devil, and then by the description of the odious Zantiot woman. The central idea seems to be the cruel and inhuman behavior of this unnamed female toward the Missolonghi refugee women who were living in Zakynthos in destitution and agony. The fifth and most important chapter presents a prophecy concerning the eventual fall of

Missolonghi. The later chapters depict the horrible circumstances of this disgusting creature's suicide by hanging. All sorts of symbols and quasi-allegorical elements can be traced in this powerful prose, as well as an ample use of the supernatural: horrifying apparitions, ghosts, and the rest (II, 33–51).

To this day, nobody knows for sure exactly what Solomos was trying to satirize in this often abusive and caustic draft. One thing can be inferred with certainty, however: Solomos was obsessed by certain characters and situations in Zante of that time, and the fate of the uprooted and miserable victims of the war wounded his heart. Missolonghi, which had successfully withstood the first Turkish siege, was now (1826) besieged for a second time. The garrison had been reduced to a few hundred starving, exhausted, and mostly sick or wounded men.[3] The Greek armed merchantmen, who earlier had been successful in running the naval blockade by the Ottoman fleet, now could do nothing, and an iron pincer was squeezing the historic town from all directions.

It is not likely that the woman of Zakynthos is just another personal satire against Mrs. Robert Solomos, or Miss Messalas, as some critics have it.[4] Rather, it is a more general attack on the impersonal group of Zantiot aristocrats and on especially their women, who were completely unsympathetic to their suffering fellow Greeks elsewhere. A liberal intellectual like Solomos, Varnalis observes, was indignant at the lack of charity and compassion of some nobles.[5]

Other commentators believe that England, or rather the English administration of the islands, is pilloried in the form of this woman, and the prophecy concerning her death prophesies the fall of England, which prophetically occurred later and which Solomos had already predicted in his "Hymn." The issue will probably remain a subject of speculation.

What can be observed about "The Woman of Zakynthos" is that the idiom is considerably more polished than in earlier satires, that the emotional involvement of Solomos contributed greatly to the apocalyptic power of the text, and that his prose style is professionally first rate. Had he allowed this to be published then, or had Polylas published the whole text in 1859, Solomos would have established himself as a most skilled prose writer in the vernacular as well.

Solomos's handling of demotic prose in the "Dialogue" was another impressive document to support this claim. Unfortunately, only this prose text appeared in print before the twentieth century, much to the loss of nineteenth-century Greek fiction writers—like Alexander Papa-diamantis—who had talent but had no Greek models, or an established tradition, to follow.[6]

III   *"The Hair"*

Solomos's last attempt at verse satire originated in his psychological and mental reaction to the events that led to, and followed, the infamous trial. "The Hair," also known as "Satiric of 1833," was Solomos's missile hurled against John Leontarakis and his lawyers. When one reads the extant manuscript with its main text of some fifty-two rhyming couplets (of fifteen-syllable lines), and its numerous additions and variations of lines and half-lines (a grand total of over five hundred lines), plus several pages of prose drafts, and thoughts, in Italian, one realizes the intensity of Solomos's involvement with the trial and his psychological need to create an outlet for his pent-up emotions by means of this devastating and fiery text.

Written in 1833 in Corfu and feverishly replowed and revised, "The Hair" actually has a simple plot: The Devil, disguised as a Friar, weighs the "doctor of laws" on his scale and finds him lighter than a hair. The hair had been found in a love letter of the lawyer's mother, who is presented as a prostitute. This detail is related to the stratagems used by Leontarakis's lawyer, Napoleon Zambelis, at the trial. The man who does not know who his father is, because of his mother's occupation, tries to prove that others (the two Solomoi) are illegitimate. In the "thoughts" to the poem and several variations, Solomos took good care of Forestis, too, Leontarakis's other lawyer (II, 251–77).

This satire is introduced in Solomos's usual dream framework. To alter the over-all effect, however, the narrator wakes up to find everything that he had seen in his dream still there, in his room, which also smells of sulphur, a sign that the Devil had actually been there, too. This is a new device, for this time Solomos implies that the dream is reality, and vice versa.

The idea for this sort of judgment is taken from the Bible (Daniel 5:1). The final result, the hair outweighing the lawyer—that is, his talent as a barrister—is not reached immediately. First the scale turns toward the lawyer's side. The Devil, however, soon finds out why: a dead fly has made the difference as part of it had fallen into the same disc of the scale.

Solomos in this most personal satire shows himself at his best as a satirist. Subject matter, arguments, and imagery are well chosen and to the point. The language is far better than in any similar poem heretofore. The versification is very competent, and the fifteen-syllable couplets rhyme successfully and in telling words.

At that time Solomos was also working on "The Cretan," and he had not given up "Lambros" entirely. The same notebook that contains "The Hair" and its bulky addenda contains lines of "The Cretan." Many a reader of Solomos may then wonder if it was worthwhile to spend so much precious time and creative energy on a project such as this satire. What if all the talent spent, if not wasted, on "The Hair" had been applied toward the completion of "The Cretan," which was begun in exactly the same meter and form; or even the almost abandoned "Lambros"? The only answer is that if the poet could have disciplined his emotional world as well as all that, and marshaled and controlled his spiritual resources at will, he would perhaps have been a cooler intellectual, and not a living and natural being and spontaneous lyric poet.

Solomos wrote no more satires, in either language, after "The Hair." As has already been mentioned, a satiric poem despite its possible vituperation, is essentially a didactic, moralizing work. But who or what would there be to learn from Solomos? One can understand that when an indignant and sensitive artist ceases even to criticize what is wrong, he has become too skeptical, too isolated, and no longer involved in public affairs. At the end of the trial Solomos was forty years old, but most of his enthusiasm and youthful commitment began slowly to evaporate.

IV *"The Dialogue"*

The only scholarly essay Solomos wrote in Greek prose is the celebrated "Dialogue" (1823). Its genre is the Platonic dialogue; but the subject matter and language ideally agree with this form of prose. Solomos was not exactly an innovator in expressing his views concerning the modern Greek language in an essay with a dramatic form. John Vilaras's *The Most-Scholarly Traveller* was, at least in part, a dialogue about the form of the written language. Adamantios Koraes also wrote in this genre his *Dialogues between Two Greeks.* At the end of a large volume, titled *Hellenic Nomarchy* (1806), there was appended a dialogue, too. Essays in dialogue form had also been written by European authors such as Stendhal, Ermes Visconti, and others.[7]

Most sources of the "Dialogue" are actually mentioned, or alluded to, in the text itself. This, however, did not prevent Greek and Italian critics from writing numerous essays to prove what Solomos had borrowed from whom, when, and how. For instance, Peter Vlastos maintained that when Solomos wrote the "Dialogue" he had not read Dante's famous essay *De Vulgari Eloquentia* (Of the Eloquence of the Vernacular).[8] On the contrary, comments the scholarly Zissimos Lorentzatos, Solomos knew Dante's Latin work in Trissino's Italian translation.[9] Indeed, a careful study of the "Dialogue" reveals Dantean echoes.

When Solomos was studying in Italy, he experienced firsthand the problems that bilinguality creates for a writer. Dante and his disciples had been successful in convincing creative artists that Latin was a dead language and that the living dialects of contemporary Italy (Toscan and Florentine especially) were the only appropriate vehicles for the writing of poetry. In the nineteenth century these beautiful and civilized Italian dialects had developed considerably. The Classicists and conservatives wanted to see contemporary poetry written in a form imitating that of the fourteenth century. Monti was one of their champions. Manzoni, however, the artist Solomos admired and respected, had made the contemporary Toscan prevail, in all genres, in its living form.[10] Modern Greek needed a similar "boosting," so to speak, in order to become the established literary vehicle, not only in oral, but in written poetry and in literature in general as well. Many Greek scholars and pedants opposed this with varying degrees of vehemence.

Written arguments against literary bilinguality had been published by Italians, such as M. Cesarotti's (1730–1808) *Essay on the Philosophy of Language (1787);* and there is no doubt that Solomos had read them and was influenced by them. His "Dialogue," however, owes much to contemporary Greek sources, such as the theories of Vilaras, Christopoulos, and others.[11]

The "Dialogue" features three characters: the Poet (Solomos), the Friend (Trikoupis, no doubt), and the Pedant (Koraes, most probably). In it the young poet had the opportunity to use his considerable erudition, as well as his skill in logical argumentation, which he must have developed during his training as a lawyer (II, 11–30).

The Poet and his Friend begin the dialogue by connecting the fact of the War of Independence to the idea of the need for a similar independence with regards to the language question. "I understand," the Poet says, "that you want us to talk about the language; does anything actually occupy my mind, if not freedom and language?" The Friend then agrees, paraphrasing John Locke, that those who hinder communication among people willingly by means of artificial language barriers are enemies of truth and erudition. Thus, the importance of the vernacular becomes a national issue, next to that of freedom.

Arguments in support of the spoken tongue derive from observations of literary works as well as from scholarly treatises. For example, Shakespeare's dramas and the essays of several philosophers are quoted. Homer, Pindar, Demosthenes, Sophocles, Cicero, and many other masters also marshaled to the task.

In Act V, Scene i, of *Romeo and Juliet,* Romeo, in a monologue in front of the apothecary's, describes the oddness and decay of this man's wares in relation to the appearance and character of the man. According to Romeo, "And if a man did need a poison now/ Whose sale is present death in Mantua,/ Here lives a caitiff wretch would sell it him."[12] Solomos apparently appreciated the psychological association of outer appearance with inner depravity and decay, which Shakespeare suggested about the procurer of poison, and utilized it in his "Dialogue." The Poet compares the Pedants, who insist on using the artificial puristic (*katharevousa*) language, to those "men who sell poison to earn their living." The Friend comments that the laboratory of one such man is described by Shakespeare, and he paraphrases Romeo's descriptive soliloquy quite accurately. In the same essay the Poet answers the Pedant's question—"What nobility is there in [grammatically] corrupt words"?—by emphatically stating, "The same nobility the English words had before Shakespeare, the French ones before Racine, and the Greek ones before Homer—they all wrote in the idioms of their days."

Toward the conclusion of the "Dialogue" Solomos, in an outburst of sarcasm, ironically attributed all great literary achievements to the "divine"—accent marks, breathing marks, question marks, periods, commas, semi-colons, and the like of the ancient grammarians. You, he wrote, inspired Homer, even before your birth; you inspired, among others, "Shakespeare when he presented Lear, Hamlet, Othello, Macbeth, and the whole English people were moved." In another, fragmentary version of the same essay, Solomos followed the Socratic method suggested by the genre of the "Dialogue":

The Poet: English is made up of the Latin and the Germanic languages. Are you then sure that Shakespeare knew both of them so fluently, since he enjoyed such great success with the English public?

The Pedant: He certainly knew them.

The Poet: Not at all! He only knew the language of his people, and
        from its heart he drew all the material with which he caused, and
        still does, his nation to be moved. (II, 29)

Solomos's appreciation of Shakespeare's art is also attested to by the
fact that he translated, accurately and beautifully, into Greek the whole
song of Desdemona from *Othello* (Act IV, Scene iii, 40ff.), in five
rhyming octets and one sestet.

In the same manuscript of the "Dialogue" Solomos appended a note
with a quotation (in French) from Locke's essay "Of the Abuse of
Words":

He that applies the words of any language to ideas different from those
to which the common use of that country applies them, however his
own understanding may be filled with truth and light, will not by such
words be able to convey much of it to others, without defining his
terms. (II, 30)[13]

In the complete manuscript there is a passage spoken by the Friend
in which Locke is mentioned as the author of the idea that a man who
arbitrarily abuses language or uses it improperly is an enemy of truth
and of its progress. Locke's statement was skillfully altered by Solomos,
who retained only its spirit. The original is as follows:

For language being the great conduit, whereby men convey their
discoveries, reasonings, and knowledge, from one to another, he that
makes an ill use of it, though he does not corrupt the fountains of
knowledge, which are in things themselves, yet he does, as much as in
him lies, break or stop the pipes whereby it is distributed to the public
use and advantage of mankind.[14]

Apparently these ideas were intended to strengthen the case in favor
of the vernacular. Indeed, to further demolish the stale arguments of
the Pedant, the Poet often refers to the authority of celebrated sages
and authors whose views about language were similar to his. In this
capacity he mentions Plato, Condillac, D'Alembert, Gebelin, Martin
Opitz, Francis Bacon, and, of course, Dante. Condillac's views, similar
in nature to those of Locke, must undoubtedly come from his *Essai sur
l'Origine des Connaissances Humaines. De Vulgari Eloquentia* of
Dante, which was Solomos's bible in matters linguistic, is primarily used
to show the superior esthetic value of the vernacular by contrast to the
dead language of the past. The general inspiration and line of argument,
however, in the "Dialogue" came from a contemporary Greek

source—the writings of John Vilaras, poet, essayist, philosopher, physician, linguist, naturalist, and satirist.[15]

Solomos's allusions to Bacon are less concrete and accurate than those to Locke. Trying to find an authority to support one of his major arguments—that an author must first submit to his language before he conquers it—Solomos somehow altered Bacon's statement, "He that seeketh victory over his nature, let him not set himself too great nor too small tasks."[16] The other reference to the Elizabethan sage is more casual and rather too vague to be solely attributed to Solomos's knowledge of a specific work of Bacon. Referring to the wisdom of the people and their role as teachers to the scholars, a notion which the Pedant cannot accept, the Poet tells him with conviction: "Many have said it, many! Bacon says (I don't remember where) that there are some people who think that everything has been said; you think that nothing has ever been said" (II, 18).[17]

The most important idea, however, is Solomos's recognition of the vernacular as a starting point, as it were. The poet must surrender to it first, and if he is strong enough, he must then master it and use it as his own. This does not imply a slavish dependence on the language of the demotic songs, as some critics and poets thought. On the contrary, as Solomos later explained in a letter to Tertsetis (1833), the poet must utilize the language of the people with intelligence and initiative. He must "rise vertically,"[18] as he put it, from the levels that the anonymous and often uneducated, unsophisticated, and even naive, popular versifiers and singers had attained.

Solomos achieved that, eventually, in his poetry. Many other poets, though (Valaoritis, Krystallis, and numerous others), seldom surpassed that level, to soar higher into the realm of real art.[19]

The extant manuscript of the "Dialogue" is not complete. The key ideas, however, emerge from what is left with clarity and conviction.[20]

CHAPTER 9

Toward the Sublime

I *"Lambros"*

THE BEST WAY to approach this poem is by trying to project the plot that Solomos had conceived and intended to turn into a long Romantic work. Polylas left us a detailed account of the whole plan, divided into five paragraphs, or parts (I, 157–96). These can be summarized as follows:

Lambros, a young and brave but amoral man, promises to marry fifteen-year old Maria, and he seduces her. Maria gives birth, in time, to three boys and a girl, all of whom are abandoned or sent to an orphanage. Fifteen years later (the present time of the poem) Maria is still living with Lambros as his paramour, without her children, in utter misery. Indifferent to Maria's torment, Lambros joins the Suliot Greeks fighting against Ali Pasha. There he is met by a young Turk, actually a girl in disguise, who wants to befriend the Greeks because of the cruelty of her masters to one of her Christian girlfriends. Lambros has no difficulty seducing this innocent girl too, only to discover later that she is his daughter with Maria, for she bears on her palm a cross branded by Maria on their children before they were abandoned.

Terribly shaken, Lambros leaves the Suliots. While rowing by moonlight across a lake, accompanied by his daughter, the latter throws herself into the water. After a brief but dramatic hesitation, Lambros chooses to let her drown. When he returns home, it is the eve of Easter. Maria tries to pray; and Lambros strays into the church, where in his despair, he denies his God and blasphemes. Then he is visited by the ghosts of his three boys, who insist on giving him the traditional Easter kiss. Fleeing in terror, Lambros finds Maria and confesses everything to her. He is now honestly repentant and offers to marry her.

While waiting for a priest, Maria, crushed by the news, becomes insane and does nothing but sing and lament. Lambros runs away, wandering here and there until he reaches the lake, he plunges into it to put an end to his life of crime and sin. The mad mother, Maria, in her utter confusion, does the same, soon afterward.

The reader recognizes easily the staple elements and motifs of Romantic and even Gothic stories in "Lambros": the suffering and death of innocents, despair leading to insanity, ghosts, cemetery scenes, incest, desperate actions of the characters, and so on. All critics agree that this melodramatic work is the price Solomos paid to the influence of Byronic and other Romantic tales. The character of Lambros, they said, is Byronic.[1] Superficially, these observations have some merit.

Solomos, however, was an entirely different man and poet than Byron. What makes Byron's heroes so interesting is the projection of much of Byron's own personal traits and ideas into them. Byron creates the impression of empathy with his characters, if not even that of total identification. The same is not true of a man like Solomos. Palamas, incisively commenting on the Byronic element in "Lambros," stated: "The Byronism of the poem, more exterior than not, is not marked by the purple seal of subjectivity. Whatever in Byron's poetry derives from his bleeding heart, in Solomos is but a step of the artist who is consciously moving toward objectivity; toward the meaning of art."[2]

Tomadakis put it even more succinctly: "Solomos's Lambros strongly resembles the blasphemous Manfred of Byron, to the point that it is impossible to acclimatize this untamed, contemplative, and criminal nature. This is certainly due to the antithesis between the lack of faith of the English poet and the religiosity of Solomos. But Byronism, bravery, wandering, melancholy, defiance of heaven, and bold capture of earthly delights, a magnificent storm, was not part of the nature of an explosive but basically innocuous and moralizing Christian such as Solomos."[3] Moreover, Solomos injected the patriotic element into "Lambros," as Dimaras observed, and presented the whole as a "moral poem."[4] These are elements that place "Lambros" outside the proper sphere of true Byronism.

Polylas, and the subsequent editors of "Lambros," tried to organize the found fragments of the poem into a whole with some semblance of logical sequence. Though they must be commended for their efforts, the present organization, or rather the numerous subdivisions of the poem, leave much to be desired.

Solomos, apparently, took the background of the story for granted, so to speak, and worked sparingly on the events up to Lambros's confession of his daughter's seduction. He then concentrated his energy on the most important part of the poem, the Easter Eve episode at the church, with Lambros's spectral vision and the defeat of his resistance. The final madness of Maria and the suicides of both paramours were also left in fragmentary form.

Earlier in the poem Solomos found the opportunity to incorporate two magnificent long lyrics that he had composed around 1821–22: the songs "Brother and Sister," and "The Mad Mother" (or "The Cemetery"). These most moving and successful songs contribute tremendously toward the characterization and portrayal of Maria and toward the setting of the melodramatic tone of the whole. They are the only completed parts that are not written in *ottava rima*.

The division of the poem into thirty-one fragments, some consisting of as many as sixteen stanzas, may mislead the reader to assume that "Lambros," if ever finished, would have had no less than five hundred stanzas. But this is a gross and unrealistic exaggeration. The material of the plot is simply not enough for that many *ottavas*. The proportion of the completed parts of "Lambros" to what exists only in Polylas's account and in prose drafts actually indicates that the whole could have been achieved in considerably less than one hundred stanzas, perhaps even as few as fifty.

Knowing that Solomos was no mythomaniac, nor a rhetorical poet (like Whitman or Palamas), we should not assume that, for instance, "Maria's Complaint" would have needed more than three or four stanzas or that the description of the death of "The Martyr" would have taken up more than two. Aristotle Valaoritis might have produced one hundred on that particular detail; not so Solomos. The conclusion of these hypotheses is that Solomos actually composed most of his "Lambros," certainly all its significant parts, and neglected the details. Having sensed that he had come close to greatness in the stanzas that had kept him busy for quite a few years, Solomos decided to abandon the minor details. It seems that he was not so much interested in integrated entities as he was obsessed with some passages that satisfied his quest for the esthetic ideal.

The language and versification in "Lambros" show that Solomos's ability as a poet was steadily and rapidly progressing. After the publication of "Maria's Prayer, and Lambros's Vision," in the first issue of the *Ionian Anthology,* there was no Greek poet, in or out of Greece, who was capable of achieving anything in the vernacular that was comparable to what the Zantiot aristocrat already had to his credit.

One of the sestets in "The Mad Mother" has been freely rendered as, "Clang, clang! the church bells/ Ring through the darkness;/ Clang, clang! the echoes/ Cleaving the silence/ Give back their doleful,/ Doleful reply" (I, 179). The scene is at the cemetery, where the mad mother—a prefiguration of Maria—goes by night to lament her two children killed by lightning. Her sorrow upsets her mental balance as she begs the gravediggers not to throw cold earth on her little children, who are only sleeping, she says, and will wake up in the morning to sing and pick flowers to welcome May.

Like Wordsworth's innocent children in "We Are Seven," this insane mother, as well as the boy in the other lyric, "Brother and Sister," which Maria sings, refuse to accept the finality of the death of beloved persons.[5] In Stanza 41 of that moving lyric the boy (Anthos) tells his crying mother that, "Anthoula [his sister] is sleeping/ Indeed I tell you/ Please, stop now weeping,/ I am crying, Mommy, too." One realizes, from these offhand renditions, that all eyes would indeed be filled with tears when Solomos recited these lines, as L. Strani has recorded.

Maria comes out to pray under the sky:

> Maria comes forth seeking the solace
> Of coolness for her hope-forsaken breast;
> The night is sweet, and the full-moon's face
> Has not emerged, any star's glow to contest;
> Multitudes, myriads, they glimmer in all their grace
> Some solitarily, some others abreast;
> They too are celebrating the Resurrection
> That is mirrored on the calm sea's reflection. (I, 187)

Lambros is described entering the church and uttering his defiance in stanzas that have reminded Jenkins, and others, of Byron's rebels and Shelley's Prometheus:[6]

> Downward he cast his face, pale as sulphur,
> And in a low voice these words he hurled:
> "The Saints are dumb and lifeless; no murmur
> Comes from the tombs; cried I till the midnight wild.
> Man (despite destiny's will and design), a cur,
> Is the only God of himself; he always excelled
> In time of utter wretchedness. Despair,
> Hide in my soul and rest for ever there." (I, 188)

But are Byron, Byronism, Romanticism, and the "Graveyard school" of poets the only sources and models for Solomos's poem? The answer is no. Much of what now sounds melodramatic to us was to him then reality or nearly so.

We saw how often the death of innocents in his own family inspired Solomos to write verse requiems. We know that Angelica Nikli lived as

Count Nicholas's paramour for eleven whole years. Even the projected, but never attempted, episode with the heroic monk who was burned alive by Ali Pasha has a parallel in the case of the heroic deacon and guerrilla Athanasios (Diakos) and his torturous death by impaling and fire when he fell into the hands of the Turks. Far-fetched and inhuman these details sound today, but they did happen in the spring of 1821.[7]

On the other hand, Solomos, who knew his fellow Greeks well, did not have to peruse Byron's, or anyone else's, writings to find colorful, tragic characters. Contemporary Greek reality was dominated by proud and heroic desperadoes, whose egotism and loyalty to personal honor more than once had made them fight one another, and even, in some cases, betray the interests of Hellenism as a whole. Lambros is an almost impossible character to stomach today, but neither he nor some real contemporaries were rare then.

"Lambros" is a transitional work, in a sense, in the canon of Solomos's poetry. It is moralizing, patriotic in its own exotic way, and very lyrical, but as a critic has rightly observed, the religious spirit in it takes the form and authority of a moral law. Byron had his own code of life; Solomos was satisfied with the code of God.[8]

The existing fragments of "Lambros," with all variations and reworkings of lines, amount, very roughly, to 350 lines in *ottavas,* 200 lines in sestets, and over 200 in quatrains, a grand total of nearly 1,000 lines. If Solomos had spent his time and energy in completing the story in less perfect lines, he could have composed close to one hundred competent *ottavas,* in addition to the two complete songs. But he did not do that, for he was interested in poetry rather than in Gothic storytelling.

II *"The Cretan"*

The long and undoubtedly laborious experimentation with the subject matter and form of a poem such as "Lambros" must have taught Solomos many professional secrets. Success and sensationalism could be secured, but greatness, if not sublimity, could not be achieved through imitative verse forms and melodramatic details. To produce genuinely great verse, Solomos had to turn again to the cultural traditions of his nation and utilize improved forms of traditional Greek poetry.

"The Cretan" was written in rhyming couplets of fifteen-syllable lines, technically like those of the early lyrics "Eurykome," "The Death of the Shepherd," and others. A dozen years or so had elapsed since

Solomos first used that Greek meter. By 1833–34, the period Solomos was working on "The Cretan," the poet could produce rhyming couplets not unlike the couplets of *Erotokritos* and those of many folk songs. But Solomos was not now imitating or simply echoing. Having absorbed whatever he could from his sources and models, he now composed couplets that easily surpassed them. Moreover, the subject matter was much more profound, and the technique anything but just a melodious verse narrative.

The existing manuscript contains fragments of varying lengths numbered 18–22. It is not known if Solomos had worked at all on the first seventeen parts. Some one hundred and thirty-three lines, plus close to eighty in variations, make up the existing fragments, whose plot seems to be as follows (I, 197–206):

A young and patriotic warrior from Crete loses his whole family during the struggle against the Turks. He then leaves in a boat, by night, trying to rescue his fiancee who is with him. A fearful storm is suddenly followed by calmness, and the still waters reflect the stars. A strange female apparition, a "Lady-clad-in-the-Moon," enchants the Cretan who thinks that he has seen her before.

> A cypress-like figure light from the ocean rose,
> Whose surface she trod weightlessly, in ethereal pose;
> She opened her arms lovingly and with humiliation,
> And all her beauty could be seen, all her consideration.
> . . . .
> Methought I had seen her, way back in the past,
> Perhaps in a church painted by an artist unsurpassed,
> Or deeply carved in my memory, by my passion led,
> Or in a dream, when by my mother's milk was I being fed;
> It was a memory of old, sweet, and almost faded,
> That now stood in front of me with its force unabated.
>
> (I, 200–201).

Encouraged by the magic of the situation he narrates his sufferings to her, and the Lady

> Sweetly smiled she freeing my soul from fear
> And her eyes, like my girl's, were filled with many a tear.
> She's gone, woe to me! but on my hand that still
> Was raised, I heard one of her tear-drops spill (I, 202).

The Lady thus disappears amidst a most pleasant and mysterious sound, and the young man experiences an inner elation, a love for his country, stronger than Death and Eros. When this supernatural experience is over, the narrative concludes with these couplets:

It ceased, and empty was my soul and nature beside,
Which sighed and at once was filled with love for my bride;
Finally I reached the shore and on a sandy bed
Gently I placed my fiancee, only to see that she was now dead.
(I, 206).

The fragmentary form of the poem poses problems to commentators. They all agree that Solomos's treatment of nature is skilled and invested with symbolic meaning. In discussing Solomos's handling of sentiment, passion, and meaning, Palamas observed that the artist "achieves something that recalls the grace and sublimity of the English poets."[9] Jenkins mentioned even something more specific. The "Lady-clad-in-the-Moon" is a female form with mystical connotations like the supernatural apparitions in "The Ancient Mariner." Moreover, in both poems, the sailors are alone on the open sea, undergo a supernatural experience, and so on.[10] Though there is no evidence that Solomos knew Coleridge's poetry, this observation has some merit. Regardless of direct influences, artists often create similar works, in unrelated and widely distant parts of the world, simply because the human mind normally operates along similar or even identical patterns.

The female figure presented in imagery of moonlight (cf. Byron's "She Walks in Beauty") has been interpreted, by some, as a result of Solomos's knowledge of Plato. The dialogue *Menon,* as well as other dramatic essays by the great philosopher, have been cited as sources of the idea.[11] There is certainly merit in this academic observation, but we should not forget that Solomos's beloved Dante had presented his Beatrice in an analogous imagery and aura. Nor was Schiller's practice—"to enclose the holier thoughts and feelings of the soul in woman's shape"[12]—a less important example for Solomos, who was then shifting his idealistic orientation from Manzoni and the Italians to Schiller and the profounder Germans.

"The Cretan," as Kriaras put it, "is an exquisite hymn to courageous action for a better moral world, to a higher, a poetic creation, to an activity always related to sacrifice."[13] Through sacrifice and pain, as another critic observed, the Cretan transcends the abyss of sorrow and moves into a heavenly paradise. Though it is difficult to determine the identity of the Lady in "The Cretan," the fact remains that the young man, after the elation he experiences because of her (the personified

Idea of the Motherland? of Sacrifice? of Liberty? of all of them together?—stronger than Death and Love, and presented as a divinity), accepts the death of his beloved betrothed stoically, as he had accepted that of his family earlier.

As the Cretan hero transcended the pain caused by bereavement, because he had moved into the sphere of a higher truth, so did Solomos with this poem definitely transcend the level of artistic groping to move on higher to that of the Ideal.

CHAPTER 10

The Sublime

I *"The Free Besieged"*

SOLOMOS HAD once observed that "The Nation wants from us the treasure of our own personal thought invested in national forms."[1] If one remembers this statement as he reads the detailed and profound instructions to himself that Solomos left in his papers with the fragments of "The Free Besieged," he can begin to understand Solomos's artistic intentions (I, 207–10).

This new project would start with an idealization of patriotism, and the sacrifices that it implies, and would gradually transcend the limitations of this concept on the local level. Even that would eventually be transcended, and all obstacles defied, as man's ultimate sacrifice would be made against no expectation of an earthly, or material reward. This is somehow akin to what Andre Malraux's hero, Kyo, attempts in *Man's Fate,* in a desperate struggle to transcend the human condition and gain, if nothing else, human dignity. Solomos's hero, or rather heroes, would remain anonymous; and this impersonal group would feel and act as one individual.

The idea of sacrifice for one's ideals had occurred, as a minor theme or motif, in several earlier lyrics and Solomos's hymns. In the prose draft of "The Woman of Zakynthos" one might say that Solomos was concerned with the other side of this theme, the negative and inhuman attitude toward those who have already suffered and sacrificed much. In the draft of "The Woman" one sees a monk called Dionysios, the Missolonghi refugees, and even one stanza which reappears in draft I of "The Free Besieged."

At one time, probably as early as 1826, the siege of Missolonghi was news, sensational and inspiring, but it had not yet gone through Solomos's process of recollection in tranquillity and enrichment through the intervention of reason. Its simple original title, "The Duty," explained also its central idea.

Draft I consists of the one already mentioned sestet, four octets, and a few scattered lines (I, 211–14). The narrator, Dionysios the Monk, is mentally transported to the besieged city. There, amid images of desolation and despair, against a background of battle din, darkness, smoke, and thunder, he sees a large female figure dressed in black and begins to describe what he experiences:

> Apart stands the warrior
> With tears in his eyes
> Then slowly lifting
> His rifle, he cries:
> "What use are you, musket,
> In this hand so shaken?
> My enemy knows it:
> To me you are a burden." (I, 212)

But these racy and musical lines, in their Italianate stanzas, could not satisfy Solomos's ambition. He did not wish to compose another "Hymn to Liberty" now, nor a variation of the same theme, based on the specific events of the siege. What he aspired to as an artist, Solomos knew he could not achieve at that stage. The octets were abandoned, and the generic idea was allowed more time to mature and to emerge later in a more appropriate form.

The difficulties that the poet must have experienced with the *ottavas* of "Lambros" probably made Solomos turn his attention to the long rhyming couplets of the demotic tradition. In "The Cretan" Solomos had succeeded in creating the right tone for his poem mainly because of the verse form. A shorter form would undoubtedly have turned the poem from an almost solemn, elegiac composition, to another fast-flowing martial song. Shortly after his work on the couplets of "The Cretan," Solomos began writing "The Duty" in the same meter and style.

It must be observed here that one perhaps begins to realize why Solomos abandoned the previous project. The case of the Cretan patriot's personal sacrifices and eventual transcendence to a sphere of higher understanding would now be substituted by a superior example of the same general idea: the struggle of the Missolonghiots. And the idealized defenders would not be presented as heroic Greeks only but as ideal specimens of humanity. The new poem then, although technically thoroughly Greek—"invested in national forms," as he had put it—would also be a dramatic document of far broader significance, as the German philosophers would have it.

Solomos must have worked arduously on draft II, for he composed, over the years, not less than two hundred excellent lines, and many more in belabored variations. Again, the numbering of the surviving fragments 1 to 61, with many of them consisting of just one independent line, might mislead the reader to assume that in its complete form the poem should have been of epic dimensions. This, however, would have been impossible, since Solomos was handling an essentially lyrical theme, an idea that could not be stretched too thin, nor strengthened, on the other hand, by too many realistic episodes and details. As a matter of fact, the poet was moving from the sphere of physical experience to that of metaphysics.

The plot now took, roughly, the following form: Missolonghi is the stage for a drama of mankind. Protagonists are the Greek men and women, heroic in their resistance to the brutal forces that tempt them: weakened bodies, cruel enemies, sensual considerations. The paramount theme of temptation thus enters the stage and dramatizes the conflict in their souls. The enemies, Egyptians and Turks, threaten them physically. The women must survive the slow and torturous death of their children by starvation, and they "must overcome." The men must survive the eventual collapse of their brave mates. All of them must transcend the idea of hope; assistance cannot come in the form of reinforcements and Greek ships. And above all, the greatest temptation is presented by nature, springtime, and its demands on the flesh and spirit of the besieged. If they overcome all these, as one person—a brotherhood united by strong ties of blood and common suffering— then they have transcended and become "The Free Besieged."

Solomos, for a time, toyed with the idea of naming his poem "La Fratellanza" (The Brotherhood).[2] One realizes, by now, that the composition of a work based on such inner conflicts—for the outer ones are easily overcome—fits ideally with the theory of tragedy of the ancients and its amplification by Schiller.[3] The form of a lengthy lyrical poem was not ideally suited to it, for Solomos would have to create something on the scale and nature of, say, Milton's *Paradise Regained*. But Solomos's genius was essentially lyric, never epic.

Some outstanding lines can be found in virtually all fragments.

> The absolute silence of a tomb over the plain reigns;
> A singing bird takes a seed and the poor mother complains.
> Hunger has darkened their eyes, but on them she swears;
> The brave Suliot stands apart and his misery bears:
> "Why am I holding you, my poor blackened musket?
> You are a burden now to me, and the Saracen knows it."
>
> (I, 215)

Further along—"Whoever dies today, one thousand times he dies" (I, 217)—dramatizes with intensity the magnitude of their sacrifice, their death during the most beautiful, and cruelest month of the year.

Also scattered lines like, "Always open and alert are the eyes of my soul," and "He falls from depth to deeper depth until there is no other;/ Emerging from there invincible," despite their existing like meteors in passages which were not even outlined clearly, give an idea of the transcendence and ultimate vindication of the tragic heroes. Polylas wisely left for the end the significant line, "And it watered my soul which was then gratified" (I, 237).

The events of the trial and other mundane preoccupations of Solomos, such as studying and more studying of German literature and philosophy, took Solomos's mind away from purely creative endeavors for several years. By 1844, however, he started working again on "The Free Besieged," the poem Solomos considered his life's work and artistic goal.

He worked on it, off and on probably until 1849, before he felt exhausted, physically and mentally, from the long and laborious process. But this time success did not elude him. For his concentrated and intensive efforts succeeded in giving the poem, not a final, publishable form, but the attainment of poetic excellence.

Draft III of "The Free Besieged" is a vast improvement over the beautiful draft II. Solomos now liberated his spirit, like Milton, from the limitations imposed by rhyme, and allowed his feelings and thoughts to flow freely in unrhyming but exquisitely musical traditional fifteen-syllable lines. Content and form were, once more, ideally matched, as the freedom of the lines would express the metaphysical freedom of the besieged.

Again, the numbering of the surviving fragments, 1 to 15, some of them consisting of one or two lines, is an unfortunate practice. Solomos might have felt, instinctively rather than deliberately, that a narrative unity in a lyric of the nature of "The Free Besieged," in its new form, could not be maintained. An examination of the parts that he had worked substantially, and the scattered lines and shreds in between them, as well as the numerous variations of the already achieved longer parts, may lead one to reach the following conclusion: Solomos was concentrating his artistic and mental powers on the completion of a few, but very significant, passages at the expense of a unified and successfully integrated whole. In its new form the poem had less than sixty lines, though, as always, Solomos composed twice as many lines in variations.

In draft II of his *magnum opus* Solomos had veered toward the idea of achieving an impressive length, a size commensurate with the importance of the central theme. The dangers, however, that this policy entailed, became apparent to him in the process of composing the second draft. The essentially lyrical idea in it would have to be diluted, so to speak, and its essence spread over dozens of couplets. To achieve this length Solomos gave the impression that he was losing track of the essential idea, as it was obscured, or even eclipsed, here and there by the details and episodes that were necessary for providing bulk and a certain length. But this practice is unsound for a lyric poet, even if in the process a number of excellent couplets are composed and made to fit the over-all plan.

Solomos must have realized this, and he began to recast ideas and the corresponding images and sensations into a freer form, and around certain key concepts, as it were, within the general framework of "The Free Besieged," draft III. One of these key points was the delineation of the allegorical female figure, a Mother and a Goddess, as Solomos calls her, with whom the final draft begins:

O Mother, you magnanimous in suffering and glory,
Even if your children always live in a mystery secret,
In meditation and in dream, what a divine grace my eyes
Have so they can perceive you in the deserted forest,
Which all of a sudden has wreathed your immortal feet
(Look) with Easter Palms, the greenery of welcome!
My ears didn't catch your divine step, nor my eyes your figure,
Serene you are like the sky enriched by all its beauties,
That show in many places, in others they are hidden;
But, Goddess, may I hear at least the sound of your voice,
So that at once I make it a gift to the Hellenic nation?
Glory dwells in Greece's blackened stones and in her dry herbage. (I, 238)

Again the exact identity of this mysterious divinity is not spelled out. She seems to be a composite of the ideals of duty and sacrifice, through which the defenders will be able to transcend the human condition. The ideas, however, of Greece, liberty, and religion also seem to have contributed toward her conception. After her indirect description, Solomos has her order the Poet to sing of the siege of Missolonghi.

Fragments 2–5 describe briefly the outer or exterior conflicts: the suffering, the exhaustion, the loss of hope. Fragment 6, the greatest part of the whole poem, shifts the focus from the exterior to the interior conflict, where paradoxically, nature unwittingly offers the greatest temptation to the doomed people. The temptation is presented indirectly. In that fragment Solomos utilized most of the ideas in draft II that were related to the description of nature's magic charm, and he presented them in a unified and concentrated twenty-one-line passage.

Solomos's skill at landscape painting in verse helped him to paint the necessary Edenic scene, the Arcadian pictorial canvas that, according to Hegel, would "translate" the emotional world of the poet. It is almost impossible to even approximate the perfect melody and exquisite beauty of "Temptation" into English, but a general idea may be formed on the basis of this rendition:

Eros danced hand in hand with fair April,
And Nature found its best and sweetest hour;
From the shady bluff exuding dew and scent there came
A most exquisite melody, unheard before and faint.
Water clear and sweet, full of charm and magic
Flows and pours itself into an abyss of fragrance,
Taking the perfume with it, leaving coolness behind,
Showing to the sun all the wealth of its sources,
It runs here and there and sings like a nightingale.
So does life spring up from the earth, the sky, the wave.
But over the water of the lake, that is still and white,
Still wherever you look at it, all-white to the bottom,
With a little, unknown shadow a butterfly plays,
That amid fragrance had slept inside a wild lily.
My seer, light-of-shadow, tell us what you have seen tonight:
"A night full of miracles, a most enchanted night!
There was no breeze stirring on earth, neither on sky or ocean,
Not even as much as makes a bee flying by a tiny flower.
Around something motionless that glows in the lake
The round face of the moon merges in close embrace,
And a fair maiden comes forth dressed in its silver light." (I, 243–44)

The twenty-one lines of this most important passage are actually the essence of the whole composition. The instinct of self-preservation is the only obstacle that keeps all people from the level of heroes. Heroism, however, appears in various manners and degrees. Heroic is one who fights hoping for victory and survival. Heroic is the "desperado" who engages in a fight whose conclusion can only be death. Finally, heroic is the one who loves life dearly, for it promises him delight and joy; and yet he sacrifices his life to the supreme duty without any hope for survival or salvation. This is the kind of temptation that Solomos dramatizes in "The Free Besieged," and especially in the above passage.[4]

Like Chaucer in his "General Prologue" to *The Canterbury Tales*, Solomos utilizes the imagery of spring in all its pictorial and connotative richness. It is a beautiful day of creative energy and joy. The birds sing their sweetest melodies as they mate. The fresh and crystalline waters flow amid the fragrance of flowers, and the murmur of the running water competes with the melodies of the birds. Even a butterfly wakes up, intoxicated, from her nuptial bed, the wild lily, and playfully chases a shadow on the still surface of the lake.

Equally fascinating is the image of the night. In the calm of night the man who is possessed by the ability to have visions experiences the emergence of a most beautiful girl out of the water. She is Liberty, or Greece, or both; but as it happens so often in Solomos's allegorical personifications of his mature period, she remains a mysterious, an enigmatic quasi-Platonic symbol. She is never explained as the reader is left free to become involved and interpret her for himself. This is another characteristic of Symbolic poetry, though nobody knows whether Solomos achieved it deliberately, or because of his artistic instinct.

Three images dominate this exquisite fragment: the beauty of the April day, the magic of the calm night, and the vision of the seer (alaphroiskiotos). The logical sequence of these images is meticulously thought out and executed in the poem. Mystery and beauty create a sense of awe and expectation. For a man to deny all these, plus so many more concrete temptations, is an act of greatness; and paradoxically, a man in negating the self, elevates the self to higher spheres of awareness and spiritual existence.[5]

Following this passage is the narration of a dream by a young girl, whose beloved one had fallen fighting as a hero (fragment 8). She addresses the Angel of her vision who offers her his wings. Then she turns to the womenfolk around her and explains that she needs the wings, not to fly away, but to wait for the hour of death.

The external and internal temptations have now been overcome, and what remains is a courageous and calm preparation for the end. The details of dramatic sally *(exodus)* are only intimated, since Solomos was not writing a chronicle in verse. The three lines of fragment 13 can be paraphrased as, "The swords are ready to cut a trail among the inimical flood of weapons [that surround them], so that people may remain free; over there with their brothers, here with death."

A woman's voice is then heard: "The dry reed goes through Turkish swords and muskets!" The superhuman effort to achieve the impossible is epigrammatically translated in the metaphor of the weak but hardy plant trying desperately to cut through the sea of steel and fire around it. And "The Free Besieged" ends with the image of a light like that of the sun piercing the black and dense clouds and hitting the summit of the mountain and the homes scattered in the grass. This last sketch might have been part of a canvas "translating" Solomos's feelings about the blowing up of the powder magazine, by the few old and weak Missolonghiots who had decided to stay in the town till the moment it became flooded by the swarm of the enemy.[6]

Solomos thus suggests, but never tells, the details. The defenders had "overcome." They were destroyed but not defeated; they had lived and died in dignity as free human beings. One of the most recent comments on this poem concludes in this way: "The *exodus* [sally] from this world, the leaping over there, to the open, to the divine Beyond, must be the crowning of man's spiritual endeavor—the endeavor of a man who was and still is a 'free besieged,' in the 'existential' meaning that Solomos gave the term."[7] And Solomos had made it quite clear that these people did not choose to die to gain political freedom or admission to heaven but did so in order to be themselves.

In his scattered but epigrammatic lines, as well as the splendidly concentrated passages, Solomos manifested his unique ability to capture the moment of truth, so to speak, and turn it into verse, into pure poetry of essence.[8] What he did not bother to produce would have been the mere connective filling in adroit verse. In his technique, then, Solomos was moving away from the popular practice and strictures of Romantic verse narrative, plunging into the realm of Symbolism, which was being born in France as Solomos was slowly approaching his end as a poet and as a man. The last great Greek poem of Solomos, "Porphyras," actually reinforces this conclusion in a magnificent way.

II *"Porphyras"*

Polylas, and other friends of Solomos, insist that they had heard the poet recite "Porphyras" as a complete poem.[9] Though the condition of the surviving manuscript preserves the poem in fragmentary form only, it is unsound to ignore Polylas's statement altogether.

Contemporary newspaper accounts of a tragic accident provide details about the event that inspired Solomos. An English soldier swimming in the harbor of Corfu was attacked and killed by a shark, a *porphyras* as it is called in the local dialect. This tragic mishap occurred on July 19, 1847.[10] Solomos was moved by the realization of how a brutal and unintelligent force, the sea-monster, had thoughtlessly destroyed a young and handsome man at the very moment he was enjoying the beauty of nature and feeling himself in complete harmony with it. The young Englishman was probably experiencing a stage of empathy with the elements of nature surrounding a person, which may remind one of the Wordsworthian third, and final, stage in man's understanding of, and relation to, nature as presented in "Tintern Abbey."

The scattered lines and groups of lines that make up "Porphyras" today have been edited in eight parts. But the poet, there is no doubt, would have intended this work to appear as one integrated whole, with hardly any stanzaic divisions. Meter and form are the same as in "The Free Besieged," draft III, the unrhyming fifteen-syllable line at its best. Some forty-five excellent lines make up the whole, but Solomos, true to his artistic ideals, composed not less than sixty in variations.

According to Solomos, the young swimmer, surrounded by the sky, the sea, and the earth, seems to be expecting a kind of epiphany that will reveal to him the mystery of nature. He exists in a moment of complete contentment and is about to experience the ultimate. The moment of truth, so to speak, is offered by the brutal force, the shark, that appears. It symbolizes the struggle between our spiritual self against the strength of matter, the cruel and tragic conflict between sanctity and violence, a favorite theme in Solomos's verse.[11] In the process of working this theme, Solomos composed some lines describing the magic of nature so beautifully that they make the reader actually partake of the mystical union that the soldier was experiencing.

Rarely has synesthesia been achieved in unwittingly Symbolic verse so successfully and in such a refined and subtle manner in modern Greek verse. And it took decades before future poets could achieve something similar.

The mystical charm of nature and the hero's empathy with it are expressed in lines like these:

"A thousand stars may the night send to swim with me in the water!"

(I, 252)

> Bird, little birdie, as you pour forth the miracle of your song,
> If happiness cannot be found in the marvel of your voice,
> Then mirth has never been on earth, neither has it in heaven.
>
> (I, 253)

The lines expressing the moment of truth, the epiphany and transcendence of the young man, are also impressive:

> Sweetly I kiss my arms and my breast embrace.
> Always open and alert are the eyes of my soul.
>
> Nature, you shone in a smile, and became one with him;
> Hope, you tied up his mind with all the charms you master.
>
> (I, 253–54)

> A light flashed like lightning and the youth knew himself.
>
> (I, 255)

"Porphyras" and "The Free Besieged" are excellent specimens of the importance that Solomos bestowed on inner conflict, epiphany, and transcendence as a means for achieving sublimity in poetry.[12] Labels such as Transcendentalism or Symbolism really do not help a reader understand or appreciate an author better. In these great poems, however, Solomos succeeded in creating art that was on a level, in many of its aspects, with the art that the celebrated poets of the Romantic era were creating in Europe. Modern Greek poetry was not in its infancy any longer.

CHAPTER 11

The Swan-Songs

I *Greek*

DESPITE THE COLOSSAL effort in intellectual, spiritual, and physical concentration and energy that these subtle masterpieces had demanded, the now rapidly aging and often sickly Solomos found the time to compose some occasional pieces and even to plan a few new and magnificent projects. Also, for the first time since the years of his youthful improvisations, Dionysios tried his hand again at Italian composition, especially during the last decade of his life, 1847–57.

His readings of Anna Comnena's Byzantine historical work *Alexiad* and Schiller's esthetic theory inspired Solomos to project "Nikephoros Vryennios." It was to be a poem in which the hero, like Schiller's Count of Hapsburg, would be idealized and made to predict the bright future of the then (c. A.D. twelfth century) already degraded Hellenic nation. Polylas reports that Solomos had told him that he intended "to place in Vryennios's soul the future of Greece" (I, 257).

Dionysios worked on this project probably around 1833–44, when "The Cretan" and "The Free Besieged," draft II, were absorbing all his energies. He composed half a dozen promising lines, rhyming in couplets, and abandoned it.

Another contemporary and historical event, the Crimean War, excited his restive imagination, and Dionysios wrote an epigrammatic couplet, "The Eastern War." Solomos probably intended to compose a longer lyric on that subject, for Polylas, commenting on a few scattered lines, says that the poet wanted to present the shadow of Achilleus crowning with laurel the Greek warrior Hadji-Petros, who had become involved in the insurrection of the Greeks in Turkish-occupied Epiros (I, 261). The unhappy, for the expectant Greeks, outcome of this war, probably made Solomos abandon this most sketchily projected plan. Its few lines, however, may well have been Solomos's last writing in Greek, around 1854 (I, 362).

The future of his beloved Greece inspired Solomos to attempt another lyric under the Horatian title "Carmen Seculare." He composed two dozen unrhyming fifteen-syllable lines—by now his established poetic vehicle—which survive in three groups. The last and longest presents an idealized pastoral and idyllic, postbellum Greek world, with a pious shepherdess. The poem has something of the idealistic aura of Shelleyan visions, but its fragmentary form allows only speculation as to its philosophical orientation.[1] Its fabric is basically symbolic, and its meaning, consequently, is obscure, though the purely esthetic effects suggest a kind of mystical elation.

King Othon's sailing by Corfu (1850) inspired Solomos to compose a four-line unrhyming epigram, "To the King of Greece." Solomos was always at his best in this genre, and this obliquely patriotic poem is no exception. Angelica Solomos's suicide, the same year, excited the imagination of her afflicted uncle, who composed an excellent quintet, in meter and form comparable to those of the earlier and magnificent epigram, "To Psara." The death of Emily Rodostamo (1848) had also led Solomos to express his feelings in some ten beautiful, but not unified, lines.

His greatest Greek lyric of that decade is, by general consent, the lovely six-line epigram addressed to Francesca Fraser, the charming and idealized daughter of Sir John:

A minor prophet gazed once upon a pure maiden
And in his most secret thoughts jubilant he exclaimed:
"Even if for your feet, Beautiful Girl, even if for your face,
Lilies the stone were to sprout forth, and the sun a golden crown,
These gifts are unworthy of You and the wealth within You.
A beautiful moral world, the creation of angels" (I, 260).

One recognizes the poet who, almost a generation earlier, had written "The Little Blonde Girl," "The Unknown Girl," "Anthoula," and other light lyrics extolling the outer beauty, and suggesting the inner one, of pure maidens. This time, however, the inner, the moral beauty is expressed most felicitously in mystical terms. Thus, Solomos's idealism now enhanced by his understanding of the sublime, enabled him to transport, to elevate his subject, from a living creature of beauty, to a being radiating a moral aura: "A beautiful moral world, the creation of angels."

II *Italian*

Solomos's late Italian poems are a far cry from any of the Greek works that he had written during his entire career as a poet. They are, however, vastly superior to his early Italian improvisations and exercises.

Like the Greek compositions of the same period, Solomos's Italian works were inspired by historical events, esthetic meditations, his cultural heritage, and feelings for close friends. To the last category belong his light, and often charming, epigrams dedicated to Miss Alice Ward (1853—54), the daughter of the lord high commissioner; to Sir John Fraser, to Dendrinos (1856), and to Andreas Mustoxydis (1855).[2] In this category of personal verse we may also place the sonnet Solomos wrote upon the death of Stelios Markoras, the son and brother of his friends (1852). Nothing exceptional can be found in these poems, other than warm and genuine feelings, eloquent language, and competent versification. The sonnet, especially, must have occupied Solomos's attention for some time, as indicated by its various and meticulous variations.

The already mentioned "La Navicella Greca" (The Small Greek Ship), was composed in 1851 for a public reading, as Quartano informs us. Solomos recited his poem on August 30, 1851, offering it as a topic to the Italian improviser G. Regaldi.[3] Its success was immediate, because Solomos had again captured a moment of truth and had succeeded in communicating it in the core of his lyric, though this time he did not refrain from composing the necessary opening and concluding lines. The poem consists primarily of fifty-three eleven-syllable lines, a common poetic vehicle in Italian. Solomos, however, ignored rhyme in this poem. True to his vocation, he also composed more than twice as many lines in variations on the same theme.

The event that inspired Solomos was a dramatic one. The British government, in a rather arbitrary way of disciplining its protege, Greece, over a trivial issue, ordered Admiral Parker to blockade Greece. Parker's flagship met a small Greek boat at sea and ordered her to follow the Britisher into the harbor for inspection. A worthy disciple of the revolutionary naval heroes of 1821, the Greek captain refused to obey the haughty Englishmen. Parker's warship then attempted to board the Greek ship by force; but as the British were approaching, they realized that the Greeks had lighted a torch and were coolly waiting by their powder magazine for the British to come. Parker was so impressed by this astonishing example of resolution and spirit of independence that he revoked his order and hoisted a signal hailing the Greek. The latter promptly reciprocated with pleasantries, and the two ships sailed away, following their courses.[4]

The idealistic Solomos was deeply moved by the magnanimity exhibited on both sides, as both representatives of glorious naval traditions had behaved most nobly. The passage of the poem dealing with the "essence" of the story—human greatness and nobility—may be paraphrased thus: "It was a moment, a moment only. But there was no land, no sea, no sky, nor any God then; Liberty only . . . within their bosoms. . . They all crowded together speechless, of one mind, steady there, with eyes fixed on the lighted torch and the open sea that would soon receive the bodies of those faithful to honor. . . . And, look, the spark is near the powder, but the Englishman runs and stops it with his cry." Once again brute force had been overcome by the spirit of man.

One sees again here that patriotism was never to Solomos a narrow, chauvinistic concept. The poet was always inspired by instances of greatness; by moments during which man could surpass the low and the average and soar high to the sphere of the ideal. The reason he composed "The Small Greek Ship" in Italian might well have been his desire to communicate his feelings to as broad an audience as possible: British and Italian as well as Greek.

In the same meter Solomos composed his forty-six-line "Saffo," and almost as many in variations. This more Italianate lyric, which Palamas compared to "The Last Song of Sappho" by Leopardi,[5] has as its theme man's quest for metaphysical truth. Sappho appears in a dream the poet had as a child and describes a vision she herself had of an imposing female figure, who tells her that she will live a short life on earth but that she will be admired (II, 215–16).

Tomadakis rightly observes that Solomos had somehow identified with the tragic suicide of Lesbos.[6] Like Sappho, the poet believed that the artist can find happiness only in his creative endeavors, and not in love or any other experiences of common man. The poem ends with an apostrophe to the Bard *(Vate)*, Regaldi actually, to reveal his thoughts and interpret the meaning of Sappho's vision, who seeks "truth from the dwelling of the dead and asks for the meaning of the secrets of this and the other world." Indeed this Sappho could be a mask of the aging and ever idealistic Solomos.

A kind of thematic similarity exists between "Saffo" and the sonnet "Orfeo" (1847). Solomos in it asks the archetypal artist to go to the underworld and return with the "gift of Truth, . . . the companion of man" (II, 220). What may be inferred from the way Solomos emphasizes the need for Orpheus's return to us is, perhaps, the unavoidable sacrifice of his human happiness in the process. Orpheus's return without the expected Eurydice, which would have been the crown of his victory over death, may imply the tragic failure of the poet, because of his curiosity, which was, of course, motivated by love.

Solomos had written detailed Italian prose outlines for several poems of high caliber. "The Veiled Woman" (La Donna Velata) has already been mentioned as referring to the idealized love of the poet, Adelaide, who had passed away in 1846. Solomos, once more, conceived of the divine form of this woman in the Platonic-Dantean aura of spirituality and mysticism. It is a happy poem, however, as the godlike Form takes off the veil at the end, and "The Beloved-One appeared radiating light and smiling" (II, 229-30).

The theme of conflict between brutality and beauty was dramatized by Solomos in a prose plan entitled "The Nightingale and the Hawk" (L'Usignolo e lo Sparviere). The poet had heard Hesiod's realistic story, in which the tiny bird begs his captor, the hawk, to release him, but in vain. Solomos then wrote the outline which he intended to turn into Greek verse.[7] The hawk is a manifestation of brutal violence that resists the beauty of the nightingale's song. The little bird, in Solomos's view, succeeds in winning over the cruel heart of the killer who has caught him, but by the time the hawk relaxes his "insatiable talon" in a gesture of humane protection, the nightingale is dead (II, 230). Once again, spiritual powers win over brutality, but at the cost of the ultimate sacrifice. Greek critics were enthused with Solomos's originality in this prose outline.[8]

A return to patriotism is manifested in the two plans of "The Greek Mother" (La Madre Greca), which is thematically akin to "The Free Besieged." The narrative is very realistic in its depiction of a mother rocking her child and hoping that he will one day be able to avenge his heroic father's death. The mother feels the fight is a necessity in order to keep pride in her son's soul. By the end, she is seen ready to take the child to the battleground so that he may become used to smoke "and the smell of powder and destruction" (II, 227–28).

Solomos also reworked the Orpheus motif, in two prose plans, which help clarify the already discussed sonnet. Two other Italian poems were abandoned almost at their inception: "The Young Warrior" (Il Giovane Guerriero), and "The Poisoned Girl" (L' Avvelenata), which is a far cry from the Greek poem "The Poisoned Girl in Hades" (1833).

The nine-line fragment, "The Mystical Tree" (L' Albero Mistico), is a poem that, according to Quartano, was related to the themes of the Greek lyric "Carmen Seculare" (II, 329). Nature description is impressively done, as always, but the brevity of the passage does not offer enough material even for speculation as to the poet's final intentions (II. 223).

One general conclusion is reached after even a brief examination of Solomos's later Italian works: The poet was now capable of approaching pure poetry in competent Italian verse, or in outlines which would be recast into verse in either language. Solomos kept working at his art with dedication and commitment. His last lines were written very shortly before his fatal stroke. All in all, his work remained "work in progress," but his progress and achievement as a poet cannot be denied.

CHAPTER 12

The Aftermath:
The Legacy of Solomos

SOLOMOS'S IMPORTANCE in modern Greek literature and in culture in general can never be exaggerated. As Jenkins emphatically states, "His influence was not merely enormous, but has remained unique. Linguistically as well as poetically, he achieved his aim, for no one has a better right to be styled the Dante of the Greek Parnassus."[1]

Indeed, Solomos took Greek poetry virtually from its cradle and nurtured it with the gifts of his talent to see it mature and become full-grown and healthy. To Solomos's verse turned all his Heptanesian disciples, the famous "Heptanesian school" of poetry, for inspiration, themes, verse forms, even vocabulary. As Dimaras wisely observes, none of them could match their master in more than one of his several areas of excellence.[2]

The already mentioned poets Matesis, Typaldos, Polylas, Kalosgouros plus Anthony Manousis, George K. Romas, Spyridon Melissenos, P. Panas, and others—all imitate the diction, stanza forms, and subject matter of Solomos's verse. Even those who emulated him successfully achieved artistic heights only in some details and, often, incidentally. As a whole, however, Solomos's direct and indirect disciples and followers, in and around the "Heptanesian school" of poetry, succeeded in further establishing the spoken tongue as the only poetic vehicle. They also followed Solomos's example in acclimatizing Italianate and Western European verse forms and techniques. Above all, however, their greatest contribution to modern Greek literature is the fact that they kept the demotic tradition alive. Not only that, but these Heptanesian poets further polished and developed it, each according to his special talent, and made it more than a match for the official *katharevousa*.[3]

Poets and scholars in Athens were of a much more conservative linguistic disposition than their Ionian colleagues. The so-called Old Athenian school of poetry consisted of contemporaries of Solomos, and mostly of authors of one generation later, who imitated primarily French artists and adhered to a quite different theory of language.[4]

These writers largely ignored the popular tradition as a basis, or starting point, and opted for a cultivated Neoclassical language and style as close as possible to the Classical standards. The rationale behind this choice was the belief that the modern Greek elite could not possibly create art by imitating the idiom of the uneducated and the peasants. A Wordsworth would have recognized their mistake immediately. A narrow, however, an almost chauvinistic attitude, toward the Neoclassical form of modern Greek unfortunately prevailed on the mainland Greece, a few years after the end of the revolution.

The Phanariot brothers Alexander (1803–63) and Panayotis Soutsos (1806–68) were among the poets who wrote verse in the puristic idiom, at the time when the naturally bilingual Solomos was virtually struggling to elevate the living, spoken language. The former wrote two couplets referring to Solomos and Kalvos, in one of his longer Neoclassical pieces of easily rhetorical verse. For all their artificiality, Alexander's lines were then considered great poetry. Today they can pass as witty doggerel or museum pieces. His epigrammatic lines on the two Zantiot poets can be rendered as follows:

> Kalvos and Solomos, great makers of many an ode,
> Both of them have violated our linguistic code.
> Lofty ideas, however, expressed in poor diction,
> Are not destined to stay long in the literary tradition.[5]

One can understand how wrong Soutsos was, and how his talent was wasted in an artificial, unspoken idiom. It is reported that when once Soutsos visited Corfu, he thought of calling on Solomos: "Whom shall I announce?" asked the poet's servant. "Soutsos the poet," replied the purist. Solomos's footman went in and promptly came back to the door to tell the Athenian, "His excellency desires me to say that he has not heard of any poet Soutsos."[6] Even if this anecdote is not true, it is, nonetheless, very likely the answer that a poet and a man like Solomos would have given to a versifier of Soutsos's caliber.

The purists' resistance to the language of the people was not destined to be eternal, if we may here paraphrase Soutsos's own words. Even while they were producing their rigid verse, and scholars and pedants were doing their best to spread the use of the *katharevousa*, Solomos's lyrics began to appear in the Greek periodical press and in verse collections, after they had triumphed in the Heptanese. The half-dozen or so most popular of his lyrics had been printed and reprinted some fifty times in over twelve different books and magazines. The "Hymn to Liberty" and parts of "Lambros" and the Byron poem had been published more than ten times in half a dozen European languages.[7]

Comments about the poetry of Solomos had started appearing in Greek, Italian, French, British, and German scholarly and popular sources as early as 1824 and especially after his death, in the late 1850's and later.[8] When King Othon decorated the poet in 1849, he was simply recognizing officially an artist whose impact had begun to be felt even in tradition-bound and conservative Athens.

The battle, however, between *katharevousa* and the demotic lasted for at least one generation after Solomos's death. Hellenism was in no position to surrender to Solomos's poetic theory and practice immediately. After the union of the Heptanese with Greece (1864), the situation began to change a little more rapidly. By 1880 the leading poets of greater Greece were supporters of the vernacular. The members of the "New Athens school" of poetry were all demoticists.[9]

It is impossible to trace the influence of Solomos on later poets of distinction, like Kostes Palamas (1859–1943), in just a paragraph; but when Palamas used as the title of one of his collections *The Eyes of My Soul* (1892), one recognizes immediately Solomos's line from "Porphyras" or "The Cretan." Even Angel Sikelianos, as late as 1910, turned to Solomos for *Alaphroiskiotos*, the title of one of his own verse collections, and that word reminds us of the prophetic fey, "light-of-shadow," in Solomos's poem "Temptation" of "The Free Besieged." Nor would it be an exaggeration if one were to state that no major poet of Greece, during the late nineteenth and early twentieth centuries, had not been affected, in one way or the other, by Solomos's achievement.

In prose, developments were much slower. By the time Solomos's prose began to be published and discussed seriously as literature, it was the beginning of the twentieth century, and prose writers had already learned the value of the demotic the hard way.

Solomos's achievement as an artist can be understood best on the basis of a comparison with the British Romantic poets. This should not imply any direct or indirect influence on the part of Wordsworth, Coleridge, Byron, Shelley, and Keats, or the American poet Poe. Only Byron's poetry was definitely known to Solomos. With the others Solomos had some artistic and idiosyncratic similarities, in some aspects of their art, never with their art as a whole.

Solomos, for instance, like Wordsworth, was obsessed by the

necessity of using the language of simple folk in verse composition. And as Wordsworth explains, in the 1800 "Preface" to the *Lyrical Ballads,* the language of the common people should be adjusted and corrected to fit the themes that the poet wanted to dramatize. Isn't that what Solomos meant when he wrote that the poet must first surrender to the language of the people and then master it? Isn't that what he wrote Tertsetis, when he mentioned that the poet should elevate the level of the language—"rise vertically"—to the height that is demanded by the subject? It is in keeping with Wordsworth's thought, as is Solomos's preoccupation with pastoral subjects in his early lyrics.

Wordsworth wrote about country folk and their sorrows and joys. He also wrote about the experiences of innocent children and bereft mothers. Solomos composed poems on similar subjects, not because he was imitating Wordsworth, of all poets, but because as a genuine Romantic poet he knew he had to turn to nature and to the people to find true and unadulterated emotions and feelings to turn into art.

Wordsworth had variously defined poetry as "coming from emotion recollected in tranquillity" and as being "the spontaneous overflow of powerful feelings."[10] Powerful feelings, love for country, and compassion for those who suffer actually inspired a substantial number of Solomos's lyrics, plus his "Hymn to Liberty" and the Byron requiem. One may even add here that if Solomos had known Wordsworth's theory and had adhered to it, he would have been able to liberate himself from the anguish and frustration of serious study and would have allowed his poetic instinct more freedom. Unlike the Englishman, however, Solomos never would have attempted anything as personal and long as *The Prelude.* Nor were the existing circumstances in Greece such that could have inspired Solomos to write a "Michael" or a "Leech-Gatherer." The Industrial Revolution was not to affect Greece, or the Heptanese, before 1900 or even later.

Ideological similarities between Solomos and Shelley were mentioned by Palamas.[11] Both were Platonists of sorts; both worshiped freedom, not only on the political and national levels, but on the personal and the metaphysical as well; both were revolutionaries and reformers; both were moved by human suffering; and both had considered the function of the poet as much more than the mere creation of art. Solomos would have signed his name under Shelley's "A Defence of Poetry" without hesitation. Shelley ended his essay with the statement:

Poets are the hierophants of an unapprehended inspiration; the mirrors of the gigantic shadows which futurity casts upon the present; the words which express what they understand not; the trumpets which sing to the battle and feel not what they inspire; the influence which is moved not, but moves. Poets are the unacknowledged legislators of the world.[12]

One arrives at the same kind of conclusion as he reads Solomos's "Thoughts" to his "Free Besieged." Solomos's whole life as a poet was that of "an unacknowledged legislator of the world." He preached patriotism, humanism, and a higher sense of morality. Like Shelley's poet, he was a prophet, he saw the future in his visions, he predicted the proper developments, and, like Shelley, he worked for them. Unlike Shelley, however, Solomos could not afford to speculate about the metaphysical condition of mankind as a whole, at a time when his beloved and tiny Greek world was the sole center that attracted his attention. Nor could Solomos toy with the idea of atheism, as Shelley had done, since he profoundly believed in a Divine Being that made man's existence meaningful. "If there is no God, what is there?" Solomos once asked,[13] and he was not so sure, as Shelley, that man could take God's place. Contemporary man, for Solomos, was far from being Prometheus.

Solomos's similarity with Coleridge has really little to do with what was mentioned by Jenkins: the supernatural element in verse, and drink or drug addiction in life, plus "half-baked metaphysics."[14] Solomos's philosophical inclinations actually helped him achieve profundity and attain the desired sublimity in his art. Similarly, Coleridge's development as a profound critic and esthetic philosopher is not something that can be dismissed as "half-baked metaphysics," even if it was achieved at a high price. Nor is quantity what counts in poetic creation more than quality, even if the latter appears in fragments and scattered lines. Now unlike Coleridge, Solomos would never have written narratives like "The Ancient Mariner" and especially in its archaic diction. Nor would he have attempted anything so personal as "Dejection: An Ode."

Similarly, Solomos would not have much use for lengthy lyrical epics like Keat's "Endymion" or "The Fall of Hyperion." On the other hand, Solomos attempted a Romantic, quasi-Gothic tale, "Lambros," whose spirit is not too far from "Isabella" or "The Eve of St. Agnes." Both poets in these cases utilized folkloric elements, significant religious holidays, plus unhappy love affairs. Solomos's poem is, of course, much more Byronic than Keatsian; Solomos, however, shared Keats's obsession with the quest for Truth, and his identification of it with Ideal Beauty. Nor are passages of Solomos's nature description, especially in "Temptation," unlike (in poetic effects and the ability to create synesthesia) what Keats had achieved in several of his great odes. Nor was Solomos's admiration for Dante, Petrarch, Homer, and other illustrious masters different from the awe that the young Keats had experienced upon first reading Homer in translation.[15]

The few similarities, and the numerous differences, that exist between Solomos and Byron have already been discussed in appropriate chapters of this study and need not be repeated here. Simos Menardos, however, an Oxford scholar, had commented that nothing was more alien to Solomos's nature than the composition of long narratives in verse.[16] In this respect Menardos saw a similarity with Edgar Allan Poe, who had stated, in his essay "The Poetic Principle," that "a long poem does not exist," only a series of shorter lyrics.[17] This theory, superficially, seems to describe Solomos's practice as well. But, as Apostolakis observed, Solomos never expounded any such theory himself; on the contrary, he was always trying to write a poem of proper magnitude.[18] "The Cretan," "Lambros," and "The Free Besieged" are long poems. True, the last two are episodic in their structure, a series of lyrics rather than a well-unified poetic text, but they are entirely different from what the American Romantic had ever achieved.

Poe was primarily interested in the external elements of good poetry (versification, language, melody); Solomos, on the contrary, was seeking artistic and moral sublimity in content; though, of course, he was meticulously working on the external elements as well.

This comparison and contrast of the Greek poet and his contemporaries outside Greece can be extended to include Germany's Goethe. Though Solomos's lyric "To a Nun" may have been influenced or inspired by *Faust*, the similarity again is neither idiosyncratic nor specific in literary terms. Bishop Nicholas Katramis, as well as Tommaseo, had mentioned a similarity in the magnificent physical appearance of the two artists.[19] Though there is no concrete evidence for the legend that Goethe had hailed Solomos as the Byron of Greece, the best description of what a Poet of his Nation is came from Goethe and, indeed, fits Solomos's case perfectly. The National Poet, according to Goethe, appears

When he finds in the history of his nation great events and their consequences in a felicitous and significant unity. When he does not seek in vain for greatness in the souls of his compatriots, for depth in their feelings, for strength and consequences in their actions. When he himself, saturated in the national spirit, feels, with the genius which lies within him, that he is capable of loving the past in the same way as the present.[20]

Solomos, in his major works, proved that he was capable of all these stipulations. The passing of time has not, paradoxically, been able to date Solomos's verse. Today his lyrics are as fresh and popular as they were a century and a half ago.[21] The "mixed but legitimate" genre, that Solomos had sought and achieved, is perhaps the reason why his poetry can always be considered as a bridge connecting today with yesterday. C. A. Trypanis, of Oxford and the University of Chicago, quite epigrammatically summed up the importance of Solomos in the following lines: "He is a figure outstanding in the whole of European literature because he finally succeeded in combining harmoniously the classical and romantic spirits. His creations attained greater perfection with every year as he mastered his tools of language and moulded his imagination by the rules of great art."[22]

For Greece Solomos was, to paraphrase the dictum about Shakespeare, not for a time, but for all ages.

Notes and References

Chapter One

1. Reghas Pheraios (Velestinlis) had published, in Greek, the following texts: *The School of Delicate Lovers* (1790), *A Physics Selection* (1790), *Moral Tripod* (1797), *New Political Administration, Thourios* (1798), *Manual* (1797), and others.

2. N. B. Tomadakis, ed., *Ta erga tou Solomou* (*The Works of Solomos* (Athens: Aetos, 1954), "Introduction," p. 25. Hereafter referred to as "Introduction."

3. *Ibid.,* p. 12.

4. Sir Romilly Jenkins's translation of *tabakieris,* in *Dionysius Solomos* (Cambridge: At the University Press, 1940), p. 6.

5. E. Kriaras, *Dionysios Solomos* (Athens: Hestia, 1969), pp. 12-13.

6. "Introduction," p. 46.

7. Solomos as a family name was not uncommon in Crete, Cephalonia, Corfu, Corinthia, Ithaka, Monemvasia, Zante, the Cyclades, Odessa, and elsewhere. *Ibid.,* p. 11.

8. To name a few, new and old: Mario Vitti, F. M. Pontani, Bruno Lavagnini, G. Canna, V. Biagi, G. Barone, G. Regaldi, N. Tommaseo, T. Semmola, G. Montani, P. Ciuti, F. Orioli.

9. Toynbee calls Solomos "The Italian poet Dionisio Salomone" and tries to present him as a Hellenized Italian rather than as a Westernized Greek, belittling, in the process, the poet and the culture of modern Greece. Toynbee's anti-Greek bias is manifested in most of his writings. When he was writing the Solomos piece, Greece and England were rivals over Cyprus, and this might have enhanced Toynbee's antipathy for the nationalist Greek poet. See his, *A Study of History* (Oxford University Press, 1954), VIII, "The Conflict of Cultures in the Soul of Solomos," pp. 679-80.

10. Kriaras, p. 11.

11. For various aspects of the language question in modern Greece see: K. Th. Dimaras, *Historia tes Neohellenikes Logotechnias (A History of Neo-Hellenic Literature)* (Athens: Ikaros, 1968), pp. 39, 49, 54, 57, 60, 62, 67, 89, 91, 95, 100-6, 110, 114, 159, 178, 266, 357, 430, 515, and *passim.*

12. Jenkins, pp. 4-6, 48-51.

13. *Ibid.,* pp. 49-51.

14. *Ibid.,* pp. 6, 48.

15. "Introduction," pp. 23-25.

16. Leslie A. Marchand, *Byron, A Biography* (New York: Knopf, 1957), pp. 675, 706, 777, 808, 818, and *passim*.

17. Jenkins, p. 12.

18. See: "Introduction," pp. 27-28. Kriaras, p. 140 (note).

19. Jenkins, p. 9. Dinos Konomos in his *Solomika (Solomoniana)* (Athens, 1963), p. 7, mentions the existing churches. Jenkins apparently mistook St. Paraskeve for Our Lady. Jenkins's study is often marred by factual inaccuracies.

20. Kriaras, p. 14.

21. "Introduction," p. 27.

22. *Ibid.*, p. 25. Jenkins, pp. 13-14.

23. Kriaras, p. 14.

24. *Ibid.*, p. 15. J. Polylas, "Prolegomena," in D. Solomou *Hapanta (Complete Works)* (Athens: Ikaros, 1961), I, 10. Hereafter cited as "Prolegomena." The text is edited by L. Polites.

25. B. Bellini, *Callomazia; Poema estetico-didascalico sul bello* (Milano, 1841), p. 42.

26. Kriaras, p. 16.

27. Linos Polites, *Ho Solomos sta grammata tou (Solomos Through His Letters)* (Athens: Hestia, n. d.), pp. 47-52. Hereafter cited as *Letters*.

28. *Uno studente dell' Universita di Pavia negli anni 1815–1818* (Pavia, 1896), *passim*. Kriaras, p. 16.

29. "Prolegomena," p. 12. Kriaras, p. 23.

30. Kriaras, pp. 24-25.

31. *Ibid.*, pp. 20-26.

32. *Ibid.*, p. 36. Archibald Colquhoun, *Manzoni and His Times* (London: J. M. Dent, 1954), pp. 10-11.

33. See Solomos's "Elogio di Ugo Foscolo," in *Hapanta (Complete Works)*, ed. L. Polites (Athens: Ikaros, 1955), II, 185ff. Hereafter cited as Solomos.

34. "Prolegomena," pp. 12-13.

35. Kriaras, pp. 26-28.

36. *Ibid.*, p. 29.

⋅⋅ *Chapter Two*

1. Konomos, p. 6.

2. Kriaras, pp. 30-32.

3. *Ibid.* See also Solomos, I, 267-90; and II, 159-70.

4. The names Dionysios and Robert Solomos appear in a list of members of the Society of Friends, dated 1819-21. See photocopy opposite p. 80 in *Exposition du Centenaire de Solomos,* ed. Octave Merlier (Athènes: Institut Français, 1957). Hereafter cited as *Exposition*. Konomos (p. 16) even mentions that members of the society used

to meet in Dionysios's house. All other biographers, however, remain skeptical.

5. D. Pantelodemos, "Energeiai tou Voltairou pros apeleutherosin tes Hellados" ("Voltaire's Activities for the Liberation of Greece"), *Epeirotike Hestia*, XVIII (November–December, 1969), 497-515. See also Dimaras, pp. 176ff. and 251ff.

6. "Introduction," p. 31.

7. Jenkins, pp. 27-29. Konomos p. 15.

8. Kriaras, p. 13.

9. Linos Polites, *Gyro ston Solomo: Meletes kai arthra (Studies and Articles Concerning Solomos)* (Athènes: Collection de l'Institut Français d' Athènes, 1958), No. 105, p. 120. Hereafter cited as *Studies*.

10. For such anecdotes see, Kostas Kairophylas, *He Zoe kai to Ergo tou Solomou (The Life and Work of Solomos)* (Athens: I. Sideris, 1946), *passim*.

11. Kriaras, p. 36.

12. Jenkins, pp. 52-53. Also, *Exposition*, p. 145.

13. *Ibid.*, p. 126.

14. *Ibid.*, pp. 151-52. Kriaras, p. 65. "Introduction," p. 69.

15. Solomos, II, 299-302.

16. Jenkins, p. 53.

17. *Ibid.*, pp. 54-55. Kriaras, p. 40.

18. Kriaras, p. 41.

19. *Dokimes (Essays)* (Athens: Fexis, 1962), p. 65.

20. *Studies*, p. 122.

21. Jenkins, pp. 67-68.

22. Solomos's letter of May 20, 1824, to Andreas Louriotis in London. See, Kriaras, p. 147 (note).

23. C. Claude Fauriel, *Chants populaires de la Grèce moderne* (Paris, 1824–25), 2 vols.

24. C. B. Sheridan (1796–1844), *The Songs of Greece from the Romaic Text by M. C. Fauriel, with additions, translated into English verse* (London, 1825). The previous year Sheridan had published an enthusiastic review of Fauriel's Greek songs. See R. Jenkins's article in *Anglo-Hellenike Epitheorese (English-Hellenic Review)*, 3(1946), 280ff.

25. Jenkins, pp. 108-11.

26. As late as 1934 Alekos Lidorikis published a long play, *Lord Byron* (Athens: Demetrakos), which had been staged with an all-star cast at the National Theater.

27. Kriaras, pp. 64-67.

28. Jenkins, pp. 102-6.

Chapter Three

1. *Letters*, p. 30.

2. "Introduction," p. 64.

3. Jenkins, p. 125.

4. *Ibid.,* p. 137.

5. See, C. A. Trypanis, ed., *Medieval and Modern Greek Poetry: An Anthology* (Oxford: Clarendon Press, 1968), p. 1ii. Jenkins, p. 173.

6. As reported by Kriaras, p. 113.

7. "Prologue" to the Maraslis edition of Solomos's works (1901), p. 31.

8. K. Kairophylas, pp. 669-75.

9. *He poiese ste zoe mas (Poetry and Life)* (Athens: Hestia, 1923) pp. 111ff.

10. Seferis, *Dokimes (Essays),* p. 65.

11. Jenkins, p. 97 (quoting the poet Martinelli of Corfu).

12. *Ekdoseis kai cheirographa ... (Editions and Manuscripts)* (Athens, 1935); p. lxxxii. Also "Introduction," p. 143.

13. P. Lascari, *Solomos* (Chartres: Institut Neo-Hellenique de l' Université de Paris, 1946), p. 16. Also, Kriaras, p. 114.

14. *Ho Solomos choris metaphysike (Solomos without Metaphysics)* (Athens: Stochastes, 1925), pp. 31, 154.

15. *Gyro ston Solomo (Concerning Solomos)* (Athens: Hestia, 1927), I, 92.

16. See "Prolegomena," *passim.*

17. Kriaras, p. 116.

18. N. B. Tomadakis uses this expression frequently in his "Introduction."

19. Russell Noyes, ed., *English Romantic Poetry and Prose* (New York, 1956), p. 377.

20. *Letters,* pp. 32-33.

21. Often cited is Solomos's enthusiasm when he heard the versifier Nicholas Kokondris recite. Jenkins, pp. 78-79.

22. *Letters,* pp. 24-25.

23. N. Tommaseo, N. Luntzis, and Julius Slowacki had a similar view. See Kriaras, pp. 86 and 114. Konomos, p. 64.

24. Kriaras, pp. 44-45.

25. Solomos was familiar with the critical theory found in F. Schiller's *Essays Aesthetical and Philosophical* (London: Bohn's Lib., 1910), especially: "On the Sublime" (p. 134), "On the Pathetic" (pp. 142ff.), "On Grace and Dignity" (pp. 173ff.), "On the Necessary Limitations in the Use of Beauty of Form" (pp. 225ff.), "On the Tragic Art" (pp. 354ff.).

Chapter Four

1. Detailed studies of Solomos's erudition in Classical and contemporary Greek are N. B. Tomadakis's *Philologika (Philological*

Essays) (Athens: Hestia, 1935), pp. i-xxxiii; his *Ho Solomos kai hoi Archaioi (Solomos and the Ancients)* (Athens: Stergiades, 1943) and "Introduction," pp. 79ff and 80-81.

2. Kriaras, p. 59. "Introduction," p. 80.

3. *Solomos and the Ancients*, p. 15.

4. *Ibid.*, p. 36.

5. *Ibid.*, p. 39.

6. *Letters*, p. 20. In July 1824 a Greek detachment of 550 men, under Gouras and Eumorphopoulos, defeated a superior force under Omer Pasha, near Marathon, and forced it to retreat.

7. Polylas, "Prolegomena," p. 31.

8. Kriaras, pp. 19-26, 119-20.

9. See, *Exposition*, Tables.

10. "Introduction," p. 154. Kriaras, p. 64.

11. For lists of authors and works known to Solomos, consult *Exposition*, pp. 223ff.

12. For a detailed discussion of the influence of British authors on Solomos see, M. B. Raizis, "Solomos and the Britannic Muses," *Neo-Hellenika*, I (1970), 94-121.

13. "Introduction," p. 155. Kostes Palamas, *Gyro sto Solomo (Concerning Solomos)* (Athens: Hestia, 1962), II, 54-55.

14. P. Vlastos, S. Menardos, R. Jenkins, and John Mavrogordato. Their opinions are discussed in appropriate parts of this study.

15. Jenkins in order to press his point paraphrases freely "The Cretan" of Solomos, using Coleridge's archaic diction. In addition, Jenkins presents each of Solomos's fifteen-syllable lines, as *two* lines in English, creating thus a form and meter somehow similar to those of "The Ancient Mariner." Unprofessional practices like this have largely remained undetected.

16. Jenkins, pp. 16 and 54.

17. Konomos, p. 63.

18. *Studies*, pp. 227-47.

19. Dionysiou Solomou *Hapanta* (Dionysios Solomos's *Complete Works*), ed. M. Sigouros (Athens: O.E.S.B., 1957), "Prolegomena," pp. 104ff. See also *Ibid.*, pp. 245-47.

20. Ph. Sherrard, *The Marble Threshing Floor: Studies in Modern Greek Poetry* (London: Vallentine, Mitchell, 1956), pp. 15-26, 37, *passim*. Also Jenkins, pp. 165-70; and Polylas's "Prolegomena," pp. 29-34.

21. Kostas Varnalis, *Solomika (Solomoniana)* (Athens: Kedros, 1957), p. 89.

22. *Ibid.*, p. 91.

23. *Ibid.*, pp. 100-101.

24. *Ibid.*, p. 104.

25. *Ibid.*, p. 105.

26. Solomos, I, 209.

27. Solomos, II, 182; and *Supplement,* p. 73.

28. Jenkins, p. 21.

29. Solomos, I, 133.

Chapter Five

1. For details of the trial see: Kriaras, pp. 74-75; "Introduction," p. 49; Jenkins, pp. 149-53; and *Letters,* pp. 35-43.

2. Jenkins, p. 153.

3. *Letters,* p. 36.

4. *Ibid.*, pp. 42-43.

5. *Ibid.*, p. 41.

6. George Zoras, *Heptanesiaka Meletemata (Heptanesian Studies)* (Athens: University Press, 1959), II, 50-57. Hereafter cited as Zoras.

7. *Studies,* p. 109.

8. Letter of March 25, 1850. See "Introduction," p. 63. Polites, in *Letters,* seems to date the letter c. 1842 (p. 34).

9. Jenkins, pp. 127 and 177ff. "Introduction," p. 66.

10. Jenkins, pp. 194 and 206.

11. *Letters,* pp. 63-64.

12. Jenkins, pp. 184-85.

13. Dinos Konomos, ed., *Solomou anekdota grammata ston Ioanne Galvane (Solomos's Unpublished Letters to John Galvanis)* (Athènes: Collection de l' Institut Français d' Athènes, 1950), No. 72, pp. 11-12, 81-89.

14. Jenkins, p. 103.

15. Kriaras, pp. 99-100.

16. *Ibid.*, p. 101.

17. *Ibid.*, pp. 101-2.

18. *Ibid.*, pp. 102-5.

19. Zoras, II, 41-49. Kriaras, p. 86.

20. Jenkins, p. 201. See also K. Kairophylas.

21. Kriaras, p. 111.

22. "Prolegomena," pp. 39-40.

23. *Canti popolari Toscani, Corsi, Greci e Illirici* (Venezia, 1842), 3 vols.

24. Kriaras, p. 102.

25. *Ibid.*, pp. 103-4.

26. *Studies,* p. 169.

27. Jenkins, pp. 181-82.

28. *Letters,* pp. 64-66.

29. Jenkins, pp. 197-98.

30. Zoras, II, 71-73.

31. Kairophylas, p. 42.

32. John Keats, "Ode on a Grecian Urn." Sherrard concludes his essay on Solomos thus: "And, where Solomos' poetry itself is concerned, its broken fragments testify both to the strictness of that endeavour and to the *beauty of the truth* which the poet sought to express" [italics mine.] Page 37.

33. K. Varnalis, *Solomos without Metaphysics*, pp. 62ff.

34. Jenkins, pp. 193-94.

35. Kriaras, p. 127.

36. "Prolegomena," p. 40.

37. Kriaras, pp. 128-29.

38. Kriaras, p. 129.

39. Arnold Green, *Greek and What Next? An Address. Solomos' Hymn to Liberty: A Poem* (Providence: S. S. Rider, 1884), p. 44. Green's is the best verse translation of the "Hymn" into English. Sheridan's was faulty, and Solomos disliked it. See, *Letters,* p. 46.

40. Kriaras, p. 129. Jenkins, pp. 199-200.

Chapter Six

1. Solomos, II, 79-88. Hereafter references to pages of the L. Polites edition will be made in my text in parentheses; the first number referring to volume, and the second to page.

2. Alessandro Manzoni, *Tutte le Opere,* ed. by A. Chiari and F. Ghisalberti (Verona: A. Mondadori, 1957), pp. 5-27.

3. Kriaras, pp. 31-32.

4. *Rime Improvvisate dal Nobil Signore Dionisio Conte Salamon Zacintio* (Corfu: Nella Stamperia del Governo, 1822). The following year appeared a second edition with a few minor changes.

5. Solomos, *Supplement,* p. 128 (note).

6. Solomos, II, 309, 312 (notes).

7. For the original see Act IV, Scene iii of *Othello.*

8. "Prolegomena," p. 42.

9. Kriaras, p. 35.

10. Dimaras, pp. 229-33.

11. *The God-Child (Ho Vaptistikos)* by Sakellariades.

12. Kriaras, p. 61. Solomos, I, 347 (note).

13. John Apostolakis, *Poetry and Life,* p. 194.

14. *Dionysios Solomos: Ho poietes, ho daskalos, ho epanastates (. . . the poet, the teacher, the rebel)* (New York: Arts, 1957), p. 5.

Chapter Seven

1. Solomos's failure to join the revolutionary armies of Greece has been variously interpreted by biographers. See Zoras, II, 76-80; Kriaras, pp. 53-54; Jenkins, p. 25.

2. Kriaras, pp. 46ff.

3. Manzoni, *Tutte le Opere*, pp. 129ff. Manzoni's youthful poem, first published in 1878, was anti-religion, unlike Solomos's "Hymn." A. Colquhoun, pp. 42,44.

4. Kriaras, p. 48. Jenkins, p. 69.

5. "Prolegomena," p. 19. Jenkins, pp. 69-73. "Introduction," pp. 83-85.

6. A. Green's version.

7. Photos Polites as Kriaras reports, p. 43.

8. Kriaras, p. 49.

9. Solomos's "Hymn to Liberty" was translated into Italian by G. Grassetti (1825), D. de Nobili (1837), N. Volterra-Chrysoplevri (1843), N. Gonemi (1855), C. Sofianopulo (1951), and parts only by V. Palumbo (1909), F. De Simone-Brouwer (1921), P. Ciuti (1908); into French by S. Julien (1825), G. Laffon (1880), E. Clement, and parts only by E. de Villeneuve (1916), I. R. Neroulos (1827); into English by C. B. Sheridan (1825), Arnold Green (1884), and parts only by Rudyard Kipling (1918), R. Jenkins (1940), G. D. Canale (1861), Florence McPherson (1884), and M. B. Raizis (1970); into German parts only, by A. R. Rangabes and Daniel Sanders (1882), and L. Buerchner. This is only a partial list. See *Exposition*, Zoras (bibliographies), and Tomadakis (bibliographies).

10. Jenkins, p. 68. Also Robert Levesque, *Solomos* (Athènes: Icaros, 1945), pp. 15-16.

11. Kairophylas, p. 153.

12. Jenkins, p. 68.

13. Kairophylas, p. 64.

14. See M. B. Raizis and A. Papas, *American Poets and the Greek Revolution* (Thessaloniki: Institute for Balkan Studies, 1971), bibliography and *passim*.

15. DeKay Drake, "Marco Bozzaris and the Greek Freedom." *Saturday Review of Literature*, XXIII (April 19, 1941), 18.

16. M. Sigouros, "Prolegomena," p. 56. Jenkins, p. 68.

17. Apostolakis has but praise for this poem. See *Poetry and Life*, pp. 142ff. Also, Kriaras, p. 45.

18. Jenkins, p. 74.

19. Kriaras, p. 50.

20. "Introduction," p. 89.

21. Jenkins, p. 52.

22. Kriaras, p. 51.

23. "Introduction," pp. 88-89.

24. Jenkins's free version, pp. 93 and 211.

25. See *American Poets and the Greek Revolution, 1821–1828, passim.*

26. "Introduction," p. 89.

27. Apostolakis, p. 187.

28. Jenkins, p. 28.

29. Kriaras, pp. 52-53.

Chapter Eight

1. Jenkins, pp. 113-14.

2. *Ibid.,* p. 116.

3. *Ibid.,* p. 109.

4. Kriaras, p. 65. "Introduction," p. 99.

5. K. Varnalis, p. 104.

6. Petros Haris, *Hellenes Pezographoi (Greek Prose Writers)* (Athens: Hestia, 1969), II, 10 and 21.

7. Kriaras, pp. 56 and 174.

8. As reported by Kriaras, p. 150.

9. Lecture delivered at the Modern Greek Studies Association Symposium, at Princeton University, on October 30, 1969.

10. Kriaras, p. 59. Also, Mario Vitti, "Ho Dionysios Solomos kai to glossiko zetema sten Italia" ("Dionysios Solomos and the Language Question in Italy"). *Nea Hestia,* No. 731 (Christmas, 1957), 45ff.

11. Kriaras, pp. 58f; Vitti, p. 48.

12. *The Tragedy of Romeo and Juliet,* ed. R. Hosley (New Haven: Yale, 1954), pp. 113-14.

13. The L. Polites edition mentions, "Lib. 3°, Capitolo 1°." It is actually Chapter 10. See, John Locke, *An Essay Concerning Human Understanding,* Book III, ed. A. C. Fraser (Oxford, 1899), II, 144.

14. Chapter XI: "Of the Remedies of the Foregoing Imperfections and Abuses of Words," *Ibid.,* II, 149.

15. Jenkins, p. 63.

16. See Essay XXXVIII: "Of Nature in Men," *Bacon's Essays,* ed. R. Whately (New York, 1857), p. 367. Also K. Palamas, *Concerning Solomos,* II, 119.

17. Bacon's *Works,* IV, 59-60; or III, 290; and VI, 433-34. Also Jenkins, p. 15.

18. *Letters,* p. 32.

19. I. M. Panayotopoulos, *Ta prosopa kai ta keimena (Personalities and Texts)* (Athens: Hestia, n. d.), VI, 78-80.

20. Solomos's critical commentary entitled "Ideas on Schiller's Ballad 'The Count of Hapsburg,'" his "Thoughts" on "The Free Besieged," his explanation of lyric poetry, and his incisive comments in the Foscolo eulogy, all written in Italian prose, were not meant as literary criticism per se. They were primarily intended for Solomos's own benefit.

Chapter Nine

1. Kriaras, pp. 77-78. Dimaras, p. 237. Zoras, I, 67. Sherrard, p. 14. Palamas, pp. 54-55. Jenkins, pp. 16 and 134.

2. *Concerning Solomos,* p. 55.

3. "Introduction," p. 155.

4. *Ionian Anthology* (January, 1834), pp. 24-29.

5. In an essay in *Anglo-Hellenic Review,* III (1948), No. 9, pp. 281-84, John Mavrogordato wondered whether Wordsworth's "The Thorn" was known to Solomos when he was composing "Brother and Sister." Though there is some sort of similarity in general theme, atmosphere, and tone between the two poets when they wrote about simple folk, the stanzaic forms and meters of the Englishman were alien to Solomos. We know how observant Solomos was and compassionate with the sorrow of mothers.

6. "Introduction," p. 155. Jenkins, p. 139.

7. For a more detailed discussion of the Byronism in "Lambros" see "Solomos and the Britannic Muses." *Neo-Hellenika,* I (1970), 110-17.

8. Panayotopoulos, I, 178.

9. As reported by Kriaras, p. 83.

10. Jenkins, pp. 143-48.

11. Andreas Horwath's essay (1921) as reported by Kriaras, p. 155 (note).

12. Jenkins, p. 147.

13. Kriaras, p. 82.

Chapter Ten

1. *Letters,* p. 32.

2. Kriaras, p. 90.

3. Solomos had read J. C. F. von Schiller's *Naive and Sentimental Poetry, And On The Sublime; Two Essays.* Trans. with Introd. and Notes by J. A. Elias (New York: F. Ungar, 1967).

4. G. N. Kalamatianos, *Aisthetikes analyseis neohellenikon logotechnimaton (Aesthetic Analyses of Neo-Hellenic Literary Texts)* (Athens: Hestia, 1951), pp. 50-55, *passim.*

5. *Ibid.*

6. Christos Kapsalis applied the torch to the powder.

7. Dimis Apostolopoulos in his essay on Solomos, *Nea Hestia* (Christmas, 1957), 159.

8. Menas Demakis, "To apospasmatiko ergo tou Solomou" ("The Fragmentary Work of Solomos"), *Nea Hestia* (Christmas, 1964), 83-90. The best essay on Solomos's poetic practice so far.

9. "Prolegomena," p. 39.

10. Solomos, I, 251 and 357ff.

11. Kriaras, p. 98.

12. Sherrard mentions transcendence, pp. 36-37.

Chapter Eleven

1. See "Solomos and the Britannic Muses" *Neo-Hellenika*, I (1970), 94-121, for details.

2. Mustoxydis, whom Solomos had first met in Italy, was the scholar that Capo d'Istria had appointed, years before, as principal of the first Greek high school after the revolution.

3. Kriaras, pp. 107-8.

4. Jenkins, p. 192.

5. *Concerning Solomos*, II, 102-3.

6. "Introduction," p. 126.

7. Kriaras, p. 110.

8. Varnalis and Michalopoulos, as reported by Kriaras, p. 110.

Chapter Twelve

1. Jenkins, p. 176.

2. Dimaras, p. 289.

3. *Ibid.*, pp. 289-98.

4. *Ibid.*, pp. 271-88. C. A. Trypanis, pp. xlix-li.

5. From *Panorama tes Hellados (Panorama of Greece)* (Nauplion, 1833).

6. Jenkins, p. 178.

7. Consult bibliographical data in *Solomos*, I, 323-25 (notes).

8. Cf. *Revue Encyclopédique* (Paris, 1824); I. R. Neroulos's *Cours de Littérature Grecque Moderne* (Paris, 1827); N. Tommaseo's article in *Il Diritto* (1856); Countess Dora d' Istria's (Helen Ghikas) comments in *Revue des Deux Mondes* (1858); T. Semmola's, *Il Conte Dionisio Solomos* (Napoli, 1858); and numerous others, in several languages.

9. Trypanis, p. liv.

10. *The Poetical Works of Wordsworth*, eds. Th. Hutchinson and E. de Selincourt (London: Oxford University Press, 1960), pp. 740 and *passim*.

11. *Concerning Solomos,* II, 65, 100-101.

12. *English Romantic Poetry and Prose,* ed. R. Noyes, p. 1112.

13. Apostolakis, p. 239. Anecdotes on the poet's religious feeling can be found also in Kairophylas, p. 555; in the "Prolegomena" by M. Sigouros, p. 113; and in all biographers.

14. Jenkins, pp. 147-48.

15. Cf. Keats's "Ode to a Nightingale" and the sonnet "Upon First Looking into Chapman's Homer."

16. "Dyo Zakynthenoi poietai" ("Two Zantiot Poets"), *Panathenaia,* I (1910), 19.

17. *The American Tradition in Literature,* eds. S. Bradley *et al.* (New York, 1957), I, 695.

18. Apostolakis, p. 94. Professor Menardos apparently had misunderstood Solomos's theory of poetry. He also objected to Solomos's dictum that the Nation must consider as National whatever is True. See John Sykoutris, *Meletai kai arthra (Studies and Articles)* (Athens: Aigaion, 1956), p. 335.

19. "Introduction," p. 76.

20. As reported by P. Prevelakis in *Nikos Kazantzakis and His Odyssey,* trans. Ph. Sherrard (New York: Simon and Schuster, 1961), pp. 175-76 (notes).

21. See Th. A. Sophokleous's article in *Kypriaka Grammata (Cypriot Literature* (1952), p. 201. Also Zoras, II, ll (note).

22. Trypanis, p. liii.

Selected Bibliography

PRIMARY SOURCES

Books by Dionysios Solomos

Rime Improvvisate (Poetic Improvisations). With L. Strani's Epistle to Ugo Foscolo. Corfu: Governo, 1822. Second edition, 1823.

Hymnos eis ten Eleutherian. Inno alla Libertà (Hymn to Liberty). Trans. G. Grassetti. Missolonghi, 1825. Bilingual.

Inno alla Libertà. Trans. Domenico de Nobili. Corfu: Governo, 1837 (1875).

Inno alla Libertà. Trans. N. Volterra Count Chrysoplevri. Corfu: Governo, 1843.

Inno alla Libertà. Trans. N. Gonemi. Corfu, 1885.

Inno alla Libertà. Trans. Cesare Sofianopulo. Trieste, 1951.

Carme Lirico per la morte di Lord Byron. Trans. Angelica B. Palli. Livorno: F. Vigo, 1866.

"Dithyrambe sur la Liberté." Trans. Stanislas Julien, *Chants populaires de la Grèce moderne*, ed. C. Claude Fauriel. Paris, 1825. Vol. II, 435-88. Bilingual. As offprint, too.

Hymne à la Liberté. Trans. Gustave Laffon. Paris: A. Hennuyer, 1880. Bilingual.

"Hymne à la Liberté." Trans. Eugène Clément, in *Grecia*. Paris.

"Hymn to Liberty." Trans. Charles B. Sheridan, in *The Songs of Greece from the Romaic Text*, ed. C. Fauriel. London, 1825. Pp. 249-88.

Hymn to Liberty. Trans. Arnold Green. Providence: S. S. Rider, 1884.

"The Greek National Anthem." Trans. Rudyard Kipling, *A Choice of Kipling's Verse*, ed. T. S. Eliot. London, 1945. Seven stanzas.

Ta Euriskomena (The Found Remains), eds. J. Polylas and P. Quartano. Corfu, 1859. Contains Polylas's "Prolegomena."

Hapanta (Complete Works), introd. by S. DeBiasi. Zante: S. Raftanis, 1880

Hapanta ta Euriskomena (The Complete Found Remains), introd. by K. Palamas. Athens: Maraslis, 1901. Second edition, 1921.

Anekdota Erga (Unpublished Works), ed. and introd. by Kostas Kairophylas. Athens: Sideris, 1927. Second edition, 1939.

Hapanta (Complete Works), ed. Linos Polites. Athens: Ikaros, 1948-60. 2 vols. I—*Poiemata (Poems)*; II—*Peza kai Italika (Prose and*

Italian Works), and *Supplement (Translations)* to Vol. II. Second edition of Vol. I, 1961.

Ta Erga (The Works), introduction, annotation, classification by N. B. Tomadakis. Athens: Aetos, 1954. Contains a scholarly and detailed "Introduction."

Hapanta (Complete Works), ed. and "Prolegomena" by Marinos Sigouros. Athens: O. E. S. B., 1957.

Autographa Erga (Autograph Works), ed. Linos Polites. 2 vols. Thessaloniki: The University Press, 1964. I—Photocopies; II—Typographic Transcription.

Secondary Sources

The special Solomos issues of these magazines: *Anglo-Hellenike Epitheorese (Anglo-Hellenic Review)*. April, 1948.

Hellenike Demiourgia (Hellenic Creation). April 15, 1948.

Nea Hestia, Christmas, 1957; and Christmas, 1964.

Heptanesiaka Phylla (Heptanesian Pages). December, 1957.

Essays on versification, language, themes, esthetics, life, and history of Solomos and his era, by various scholars.

APOSTOLAKIS, JOHN. *He poiese ste zoe mas (Poetry and Life)*. Athens: Hestia, 1923.

————. *Ta tragoudia mas (Our Songs)*. Athens: Hestia, 1934. Both studies contain critical evaluations of Solomos's works made with excellent taste in a new-critical, formalistic approach. The author is often too enthusiastic, or unfair to other poets.

BARONE, GIUSEPPE. *Dionisio Solomos, poeta e scrittore greco e italiano*. Napoli, 1910. A scholarly discussion of the poet's works divided into patriotic and heroic songs, satires, love songs and idylls, translations, and the essays on language. The analysis of the "Hymn" is particularly good.

BRADENBURG, JOHAN. *Solomos et l' Italie*. Rotterdam, 1935. Discusses Solomos's Italian works and the influence of Italian culture in general.

CANNA, GIOVANNI. *Dionisio Solomos*. Milano, 1899. A brief but sound evaluation of the poet and his work.

COMMITTEE. *Lettere Inedite*. Padua, 1852. Contains letters addressed to Maria Petrettini by Cesarotti, Pindemonte, M. Pieri, and others. Some felt, even in 1852, that Solomos was the greatest poet of modern Greece.

————. *Gyro sto Solomo (Concerning Solomos)*. 2 vols. Athens: Hestia Vivliou, 1927. Second edition, 1960—62.

ECONOMIDES, D. *Dionisie Solomos, 1798—1857*. Bucuresti: Nationale, 1946. A brief general evaluation, accompanied by verse translations of eleven poems into Rumanian.

HADJIYAKOUMIS, E. K. *To neohellenikon stoicheion eis ten poiesin tou Dionysiou Solomou (The Neo-Hellenic Element in the Poetry of D. S.)* Athens, 1969. A treatise on the importance of the demotic folk-song tradition in the development of Solomos's art. The works of the Greek poets before him are also discussed as sources and models. A serious, scholarly study.

JENKINS, ROMILLY. *Dionysius Solomos.* Cambridge: University Press, 1940. The first book-length study of Solomos in English based on not always reliable Greek and other sources. It is marred by a complete absence of documentation and bibliographical references. Jenkins is at his best as a formalist critic of Solomos's works. His translations, melodious and rhyming, are very free and often inaccurate.

KAIROPHYLAS, KOSTAS. *He zoe kai to ergo tou Solomou (The Life and Work of Solomos).* Athens: Sideris, 1946. It contains all the Greek texts with an introduction, notes, and several essays. A useful source of biographical data, anecdotes, and the like, which, however, are seldom documented.

KONOMOS, DINOS. *Solomika (Solomoniana).* Athens: Zantiot, 1963. An interesting collection of biographical and historical data which help re-create Solomos's life, especially in Zante. Most entries are adequately documented.

——. *Ed. Solomou anekdota grammata ston Ioanne Galvane (Unpublished Letters of Solomos to John Galvanis).* Athènes: Institut Français, 1950. A unique bilingual edition of thirteen letters sent to Solomos's lawyer and friend during the trial, containing very interesting biographical and idiosyncratic information.

KRIARAS, EMMANUEL. *Dionysios Solomos: Ho vios, to ergo. (Dionysios Solomos: His Life and Work).* Athens: Hestia, 1969. The best monograph on the poet, his work, and his times. It discusses the critical views and comments of all major scholars with clarity and scholarly insight. Profusely documented, and up-to-date.

LASCARI, POLYHYMNIA. *Solomos.* Chartres: Institut Néo-Hellénique, 1946. A brief discussion of Solomos's idealistic orientation with emphasis on Platonic influence in his major works. Not a book for the layman.

LEVESQUE, ROBERT. *Solomos: Introduction, Prose et Poèmes.* Athènes: Icaros, 1945. A good general introduction based on Greek sources, accompanied by translations of four major works with brief critical comments.

MERLIER, OCTAVE. ED. *Exposition du Centenaire de Solomos.* Athènes: Institut Français, 1957. A rich bilingual collection of lists of pictorial material, and historical, biographical, and bibliographical information related to Solomos, his works, friends, relatives, influences, editions, manuscripts, history, and so on. A valuable source.

PANAYOTOPOULOS, I. M. *Ta prosopa kai ta keimena (Personalities and Texts).* Athens: Hestia, n. d. Sixth volume. It contains lucidly written essays on the Romantic movement in Greece, Solomos's position in it, compared or contrasted to those of other poets of that period. Panayotopoulos's insights are brilliant, and his evaluations very sound.

POLITES, LINOS. *Gyro ston Solomo: Meletes kai arthra (Studies and Articles Concerning Solomos).* Athènes: Institut Français, 1958. An excellent collection of essays covering backgrounds, influences, biography, various editorial problems, and chronology. A valuable book, profusely documented and annotated.

————. *Ho Solomos sta grammata tou (Solomos Through His Letters).* Athens: Hestia, n. d. A brief but most accurate biographical study of the poet, based entirely on data from his letters. Properly indexed and documented.

RAIZIS, M. BYRON. "Solomos and the Britannic Muses." *Neo-Hellenika,* I (1970), 94-121. It traces Solomos's references and allusions to Byron, Milton, Gray, Locke, Bacon, and Shakespeare; it speculates about affinities with Shelley and Coleridge; and it revaluates the Byronic element in his work. Not a definitive study of the issue.

SHERRARD, PHILIP. "Dionysios Solomos," in *The Marble Threshing Floor: Studies in Modern Greek Poetry.* London: Vallentine, 1956. The author explains Solomos's poetics on the basis of a detailed analysis of his greatest works. The duality thesis, plus the absence of any comments on Solomos's "Hymn" and other popular works, betray a kind of anti-Romantic bias on the part of Sherrard. His literal translations from the Greek sound prosaic.

TOMADAKIS, NICHOLAS B. *Ho Solomos kai hoi Archaioi (Solomos and the Ancients).* Athens: Aetos, 1943. A thorough and scholarly examination of Solomos's knowledge of the classics, in the original and in translation, based on Greek and Latin literary, philosophical, and historical echoes, allusions, and imitations in his verse and prose.

TOYNBEE ARNOLD. "The Conflict of Cultures in the Soul of Solomos." *A Study of History* (Oxford: University Press, 1954), VIII, 679-80. An erroneous, sketchy, and biased general evaluation of Solomos's importance to Greece.

TRYPANIS, C. A. ED. *Medieval and Modern Greek Poetry: An*

Anthology. Oxford: University Press, 1952. Second edition, 1968. A concise and sound general evaluation of Solomos's contribution to modern Greek literature. Trypanis most expertly relates Solomos's position to the Neo-Hellenic cultural tradition.

VARNALIS, KOSTAS. *Solomika (Solomoniana).* Athens: Kedros, 1957. Contains essays and articles on the poet and his works, some of which exhibit a sound understanding of the issues. The highlights of the earlier (1925) essays, "Solomos without Metaphysics," are reprinted here. Much journalistic work has been omitted, and the Marxist biases have been toned down. Varnalis is good on Solomos's poetics.

VLAVIANOS, BASIL. *Dionysios Solomos: Ho poietes, ho daskalos, ho epanastates (D. S., the poet, the teacher, the rebel).* New York: Arts, Inc., 1957. One of the best pamphlet-sized evaluations of Solomos as an artist, a moralist, and a revolutionary, based on an intelligent discussion of several of his works.

ZORAS, GEORGE TH. *Heptanesiaka meletemata (Heptanesian Studies).* 3 vols. Athens: University Press, 1959, 1960, 1966. These volumes contain a wealth of biographical, bibliographical, historical, cultural, and philological information and data (especially vol. II) on Solomos and his milieu.

Index

(The works of Solomos are listed under his name)